BIG IDEAS
for Growing
Mathematicians

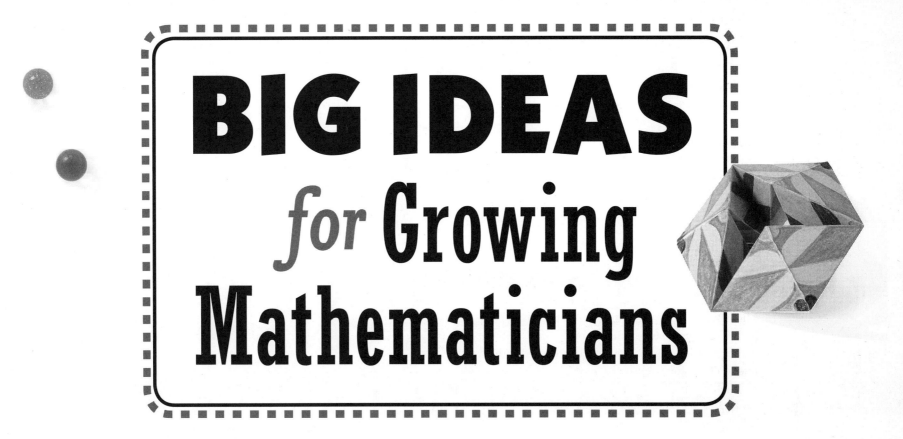

BIG IDEAS
for Growing
Mathematicians

Exploring Elementary Math with 20 Ready-to-Go Activities

Ann Kajander

Zephyr Press

Chicago

Library of Congress Cataloging-in-Publication Data

Kajander, Ann, 1960–

   Big ideas for growing mathematicians : exploring elementary math with 20 ready-to-go activities / Ann Kajander.

      p. cm.

  ISBN-13: 978-1-56976-212-7

  ISBN-10: 1-56976-212-0

  1. Mathematics—Study and teaching (Elementary)—Activity programs. I. Title.

QA135.6.K349 2003

372.7'2—dc22

2006100397

Cover and interior design: Monica Baziuk
Interior images © Ann Kajander

© 2007 by Ann Kajander
All rights reserved
Published by Zephyr Press
An imprint of Chicago Review Press, Incorporated
814 North Franklin Street
Chicago, Illinois 60610
ISBN-13: 978-1-56976-212-7
ISBN-10: 1-56976-212-0
Printed in the United States of America
5   4   3   2   1

Acknowledgments

I am particularly indebted to Ralph Mason and David Stocker, whose ideas have directly supported chapters in this book. I appreciate the mathematical support of Miroslav Lovric. George Kondor has also been most generous with his materials. Other members of the Canadian Mathematics Education Study Group have provided deep inspiration and allowed me a glimpse into the ideas that excite mathematicians. Peter Taylor has provided particular support and encouragement as always.

I am grateful to the students in my Kindermath enrichment program who allowed me to conceive of these ideas, as well as my own children, Arthur, Robin, and Maria, and my husband, Wally, for his interesting questions. As well, many teacher candidates have experimented with these activities and provided wonderful feedback. It is to these teacher candidates that I dedicate this book. I hope you will continue in your efforts to bring meaningful and engaging mathematical ideas to your students.

Contents

Students create a concrete model of a million objects to investigate how unlikely "one in a million" really is.

Students work on a collection of favorite "math magic" tricks, with explanations, for Halloween, April Fools' Day, or just plain fun.

A selection of geometry construction tasks are provided with clues for group solving.

This is a collaborative activity stressing verbal mathematical communication.

Pentominoes are used to reason about possible patterns underlying the concept of averages.

This activity focuses on developing multiplication, the distributive property, and binomial multiplication with number tiles.

Students investigate linear and nonlinear relations with a magician game.

Students investigate the exponential function with a concrete example.

Introduction

Many people think of mathematics as boring or difficult. Yet when mathematicians describe their subject, they use words like *amazing, intriguing,* and *full of surprise, awe, creativity,* and *wonder.* How can such different perspectives exist?

It seems to me that part of the difficulty lies in how we teach children. "School mathematics," until very recently (and still much more than it should), has consisted almost exclusively of rote methods and procedures. The perception is that these skills are needed before students can do higher level mathematics, where the excitement lies. This is somewhat analogous to insisting children learn to spell properly and learn all the rules of grammar before they are encouraged to write stories or create their own poetry.

This book and its predecessor, *Big Ideas for Small Mathematicians,* are meant to provide to children and adolescents glimpses of a "mathematician's" version of mathematics. While the activities do not ignore the typical content of elementary- and middle-school mathematics classrooms, they focus more on the understanding of important ideas, rather than on procedural fluency. In fact, research has shown that procedural fluency will evolve *along with* deeper understanding. The activities provided foreground the important ideas in mathematics—ideas of dimension, space, infinity, movement and change, patterns and prediction—and some contain an element of surprise. They focus on the skills mathematicians often use to solve problems—skills of working collaboratively or talking mathematics together. They focus on exploring, extending, reasoning, and in some cases justifying. Many require the important skills of imagining and visualizing. In some activities the connection to the standard procedure is obvious; in others the focus is only on the conceptual idea. Some activities are just plain fun. I hope they will provide a glimpse of "real" mathematics to you and your students.

This book is for teachers, teacher educators, parents, and most of all, kids.

How to Use This Book

Each activity in this book is divided into informative and instructional sections to make it easy to understand the ideas behind the activity as well as guide the students through the activity successfully.

- **The Big Idea:** This first section of each activity summarizes the underlying mathematical concept, so you can get the big picture before diving into the details.

- **Content Areas in This Activity:** This section lists the main mathematical content areas the activity involves. This information is also summed up for all activities in the chart on page x.

- **Process Skills Used in This Activity:** This section lists the main thinking and learning skills the students will use throughout the activity. This information is summed up for all activities in the chart on page xi.

- **Prerequisite Knowledge and Skills:** This section lists whether the children will need particular content knowledge before embarking on the activity. Most of the activities will be enjoyable for children on some level regardless of their previous knowledge and skills, but having these technical skills will make it easier for them to understand the math behind the activity. The chart on page xii lists this information for the activities as a whole.

- **Age Appropriateness:** Most of the activities in this book are suitable for all ages, with varying degrees of adult assistance. In this section, you will find suggestions for adapting various aspects of the activity to suit different age groups. For example, younger children can often enjoy an activity without having to understand all of the mathematics behind it, but each activity also allows for further exploration of concepts for older and more advanced students.

- **The Mathematical Idea:** This section describes the mathematical idea at the heart of the activity to provide background for you and to assist you in following and facilitating the children's thinking. Often children have a correct but incomplete intuitive sense of a problem, and it is helpful for the adult to have a sense of the possible approaches to use.

- **Helpful Terms:** This box includes a list of terms relevant to the activity and their definitions to enable you to review the basic terminology and concepts as well as to give you wording to use when explaining the ideas to the children. You will also find a complete glossary at the end of the book (page 102).

- **Making It Work:** This is the nuts-and-bolts section of the activity. Here you will find objectives, a list of materials you will need, preparation instructions, the activity procedure, suggestions for making the most of the activity and for helping the children through trouble spots, assessment ideas for determining if the activity was successful, and an extension activity or two for those kids who want to explore more.

- **Activity Sheet:** The activity sheet lists each step of the activity, as in the procedures section of Making It Work, but this sheet is directed to the children, with illustrations and hints to help them work through the activity successfully. A photocopy of this activity sheet will assist you in taking them through each step, although this sheet is not meant to replace your active involvement and guidance. You may decide not to use the activity sheet for younger kids who won't be able to read it well, or if you prefer to take the class through the activity orally, without the help of written instructions.

Content Areas in Each Activity

MATHEMATICAL TOPIC	ACTIVITY NUMBER																			
	1	2	3	4	5	6	7	8	9	10	11	12	13	14	15	16	17	18	19	20
Numeracy	✔	✔			✔		✔	✔				✔	✔			✔	✔			
Estimation	✔							✔				✔	✔				✔			
Scientific notations								✔												
Probability	✔																			
Geometry terms			✔	✔					✔									✔	✔	
Spatial reasoning			✔	✔	✔				✔											✔
Hundreds chart					✔															
Mean value					✔															
Area of rectangles						✔								✔		✔				
Circle measurement												✔	✔							
Multiplication models						✔														
Division models											✔									
Rules of algebra						✔														
Distributive property						✔														
Patterning						✔		✔	✔					✔	✔		✔	✔		
Measurement								✔			✔	✔		✔		✔				
Nonlinear patterns								✔			✔									
Exponential functions								✔												
Fraction models										✔										
Interpreting graphs											✔			✔						
Transformations/tiling patterns																			✔	
Polyhedra																				✔

Process Skills Used in Each Activity

PROCESS SKILLS	ACTIVITY NUMBER																			
	1	2	3	4	5	6	7	8	9	10	11	12	13	14	15	16	17	18	19	20
Reasoning	✔	✔	✔	✔	✔	✔	✔	✔		✔	✔	✔	✔	✔	✔	✔	✔	✔	✔	
Communicating				✔																
Visualizing									✔							✔				✔
Problem solving		✔			✔			✔		✔		✔	✔		✔	✔	✔			
Creativity	✔		✔															✔	✔	✔
Collaboration			✔																	
Representation											✔									

Prerequisite Knowledge and Skills for Particular Activities

PREREQUISITES	ACTIVITY NUMBER																			
	1	2	3	4	5	6	7	8	9	10	11	12	13	14	15	16	17	18	19	20
Multiplication	✔					✔	✔	✔		✔		✔	✔	✔	✔	✔	✔			
Place value/large numbers	✔	✔						✔					✔							
Mean value					✔															
Basic algebra		✔																		
Area of rectangles						✔						✔		✔	✔					
Fraction notation										✔										
Two-dimensional graphing											✔			✔						
Decimals													✔							
Applying formulas/pattern rules							✔					✔	✔		✔	✔				
Volume														✔						
Transformations																			✔	
Tiling (in chapter 19)																				✔

BIG IDEAS
for Growing
Mathematicians

One in a Million

1

The BIG Idea

Just how big is a million really?

Content Areas in This Activity

✔ Numeracy
✔ Estimation
✔ Basic probability

Process Skills Used in This Activity

✔ Creativity
✔ Reasoning

Prerequisite Knowledge and Skills

✔ Multiplication
✔ Place value for large numbers

Age Appropriateness

This activity is appropriate for all ages.

The Mathematical Idea

While babies can distinguish small numbers—for example, they can tell one object from two—older children are able to perceive larger numbers, such as distinguishing three from five or ten from twenty. Very large numbers, however, are much harder. Just how far does our numerical judgment go?

Lotteries, population figures, and high finance are but a few of the applications of math that use dazzlingly large numbers. It can be difficult to develop any appreciation of these very large numbers. How big is a thousand? How big is a million? They both sound big, but a million is much larger than a thousand—one thousand

---

HELPFUL TERMS

Probability: a fraction between zero and one representing how likely an event is to occur. For example, the chances of getting a two facing up when rolling a six-sided die is ⅙.

times larger in fact! So to have the same chance of winning a lottery with one ticket in a million as you would with one ticket out of a thousand, you would need 1,000 tickets from the first lottery! You can verify this as follows: Assume your chances of winning are the number of tickets you own out of the number of tickets sold. So if you own 1,000 tickets in a 1,000,000-ticket lottery, your chances of winning are:

$$^{1,000}\!/_{1,000,000} = {}^{1}\!/_{1,000} = 1 \text{ ticket owned}/1,000 \text{ sold}$$

In this activity students investigate concretely just how big one million is and explore the chances of winning a one-in-a-million draw.

Making It Work

Objectives

Students investigate the chances of picking one object out of a million by attempting to model one million concretely.

Materials

Materials will vary depending on students' choices of model.

✔ a small bag of rice and a scale or measuring spoons may be useful to introduce the activity

✔ calculators (optional but helpful)

Preparation

Counting out and measuring or weighing in advance 100 grains of rice may save time but is not necessary.

Procedure

1. Challenge students to think about the question of how big 1,000,000 really is and to come up with a tangible and concrete but affordable model of 1,000,000 objects.

2. Have students discuss their ideas in pairs or small groups.

3. Ask students to estimate the amount of various materials required to model their ideas.

■ For example, if they suggest grains of rice, have them do some quick counting and estimating that will show this idea to be unrealistic—depending on the size, it can take close to 30 bags of rice to make 1,000,000 grains!

■ Many ideas (such as rice) work well for 10,000 or 100,000 objects, but the number 1,000,000 makes things just that much more difficult.

4. Encourage students to make their models both affordable and transportable.

Suggestions

Since a main point of the activity is for students to devise and calculate the amount needed for various substances, suggestions of suitable materials should be withheld as much as possible. The investigation of unsuitable materials is fruitful in itself. When I first did the investigation, I was staggered at just how much rice 1,000,000 grains really was! However, here are a few suggestions to illustrate possibilities if really needed:

■ Use a computer to print out a page of *o*'s or any other character on the smallest possible printer font. Count the number of lines of print vertically, and the number of characters across, and use a calculator to multiply length times width of the characters to determine the number of characters on each page. This number can be divided into 1,000,000 to determine the number of such pages needed. Then, color in one *o* to show the "one" in one million. I keep a display like this in my classroom and vary the location of the "one" colored in; students love to search for the "one."

■ Use Internet research to estimate the number of hairs the average person has on his or her head. (It's about 100,000.) Assemble 10 people—10 times 100,000 is 1,000,000. Ask one person to volunteer one hair to serve as the "one."

Assessment

Students' models should be reasonably accurate but affordable and portable. I also like to see the entire 1,000,000—as opposed to students saying, "Well, if you had 10 of these . . ."—because it makes the activity more challenging. The "one" should be identifiable.

EXTENSION ACTIVITIES

Once students have finished their collections, they can experiment with trying to identify the winning "one" at random. For example, if you experiment and put your hand in a container of 1,000,000 objects and pulled out one object, how many times will it take before you pull out the winning object? Or will you give up before succeeding? Students can also compare this with their success with much smaller collections such as those of 100 or 1,000.

One in a Million Activity Sheet

Have you ever seen a "one-in-a-million chance" advertised for winning a lottery or a contest and thought about entering? How does a million (1,000,000) compare with other large numbers, such as 1,000? In this activity you will investigate the number 1,000,000 to see for yourself just how big it really is!

Your task is to experiment with various materials to estimate and calculate the amount of each material you would need to make a collection of 1,000,000. For example, you could calculate the number of bricks on the wall of a building and then calculate the number of walls like that needed to use 1,000,000 bricks. You could paint one brick red to show the "one" in the million. But there is a catch: in this activity, your collection must be **portable** and **affordable**. You must find a creative solution to the problem that you can assemble yourself and actually see in front of you. Estimation is OK, but remember that it is 1,000,000 you are after, not a smaller number such as 100,000.

When you have finished your collection, identify one object as the "one" in your million—perhaps you might color it. Just how long do you think it would take to pick out the "one" at random? Try it!

Be sure you can explain how you knew there were 1,000,000 objects in your collection.

Big Ideas for Growing Mathematicians, 2007 © Zephyr Press

Math Magic

2

The BIG Idea

Lots of cool puzzles have math as their basis.

Content Areas in This Activity
✔ Numeracy

Process Skills Used in This Activity
✔ Problem solving
✔ Reasoning

Prerequisite Knowledge and Skills
✔ Place value for large numbers
✔ Basic algebra (to solve Puzzle 2)

Age Appropriateness

Children of all ages can enjoy doing the puzzles. Puzzle 1 is solvable with knowledge of multiplying by 1,000. Puzzle 2 may require algebraic equation solving to explain fully.

The Mathematical Idea

Puzzles 1 and 2 draw on the notion of place value. Puzzle 1 uses the fact that multiplying by 1,000 shifts the digits of a number left by three places. The numbers used in the "magic" of the puzzle have a product of 1,001 . . . so multiplying by 7, then 11, and then 13 is essentially the same as multiplying by 1,001 ($7 \times 11 \times 13 = 1,001$). For example, $123 \times 1,001$ is the same as $1,000 \times 123$ plus 1×123, or 123, 123.

Puzzle 2 uses the fact that multiplying by 9 is the same as multiplying a number by 10, and then subtracting the number from the result: $9n = 10n - n$.

Puzzle 3 uses the fact that binary numbers—numbers that are powers of 2, such as 1, 2, 4, 8, 16, etc.—can generate all other numbers by being added together. For example, $12 = 8 + 4$ and $63 = 32 + 16 + 8 + 4 + 2 + 1$.

HELPFUL TERMS

Binary numbers: numbers that are powers of 2 (for example, 8 or 64)

One is a binary number because it is two to the power zero. (Recall that any number to the power zero is one.)

Details are found in the puzzle answers at the end of the Activity Sheets.

Making It Work

Objectives

Students are intrigued by problems that seem mysterious. They also enjoy tricking others with puzzles. These puzzles have been found to be quite self-motivating!

Materials

Puzzle 1
✔ basic calculator

Puzzle 3
✔ Magic Cards as on activity sheet, one set per player
✔ scissors

Preparation

Copy the activity sheets, one set per student.

Procedure

Puzzle 1
This puzzle can be done in an adult-led large group.

1. Ask students to enter any three-digit number on their calculator. (Everyone can use a different number.)

2. Tell students you are going to teach them a magic trick. Ask them to multiply their number by 7 and press Enter. (At this point everyone will have a different number.)

3. Then ask everyone to multiply the new number by 11 and press Enter.

4. Now comes the "magic" part. Tell the students you are going to make their original number reappear twice. Ask everyone to multiply the number they now have on the screen by 13, say "Abracadabra," and then press Enter a final time.

5. Have students compare the numbers on their screens to the numbers they started with, and ask what they see. Their original number should have reappeared—that is, if a student's original number was 123, the student should now have 123123 on his or her screen.

Puzzle 2

This is a great trick for students to try on a grown-up, such as another teacher. They can play this with an adult magician first, until they know how it works, and then they can learn how to be the magician themselves.

1. Ask everyone to choose a number between 10 and 99. (Or, for adults, just ask them to record their ages.)

2. Have the participants multiply the number they just chose by 10 and write that new number down. (For example, a person who chooses 27 should write down 270.)

3. Ask everyone to choose a second number between 1 and 9, multiply it by 9, and write down the resulting number. (For example, a person who chooses 4 should write down 36.)

4. Now, ask everyone to subtract the second number from the first. (270 − 36 = 234)

5. Have the participant tell the magician the final resulting number. (234)

6. The magician can now tell the player his or her original mystery number. Here's the magic method: Truncate the ones digit (4, in this example) and add it to the other two digits (23 + 4). The result (27) is the original number! Why?

7. Children can perform the magician role themselves once they are able to see the trick that the magician is doing. It is best to have them find the trick themselves by playing the game several times. The biggest challenge is to explain why the trick works.

Puzzle 3

1. Cut out the cards from page 9.

2. The adult can be the magician for the first time through. Instruct children to choose any number from 1 to 31, keeping the number in their heads.

3. Place the five cards face-up on the table. Children now pick up all the cards that contain that number and give them to the magician. (If they make a mistake doing this, the trick will not work.)

4. In his or her head, the magician adds all the numbers in the top left corner of the chosen cards, then tells the child the sum. This will be the child's original number!

5. Children can be the magician once they know the trick. It's also a great game for practice in mental addition.

Suggestions

Students do not necessarily need to know how or why the mathematics makes these puzzles work in order to enjoy them. Resist the temptation to tell students why they work right away. The more intriguing the mystery, the more mathematical thinking will occur.

Assessment

Students could be asked to solve, or explain, the mathematical basis for as many of the puzzles as they can. Many students will be able to solve at least the first one, but the others are more challenging.

EXTENSION ACTIVITIES

Puzzle 3 can be re-created to use six cards. The sixth card contains the sixth binary number, 32, on the top left corner. Additional numbers (up to 63) must be placed on the other (appropriate) cards for this to work. Challenge students to create this expanded version of the puzzle.

Magic Puzzles Activity Sheet

Puzzle 1

1 Enter any three-digit number into your calculator.

2 Now multiply the number by 7 and press Enter.

3 Multiply the new number by 11 and press Enter.

4 Here comes the magic part. Multiply what you now have by 13, say "Abracadabra," and press Enter. Your number should reappear . . . twice!

5 If you are not convinced, try it with a different initial number!

6 Why does this work?

Puzzle 2

Once you learn the trick of this puzzle, it's a great one to use to guess a grown-up's age. Until you figure it out, you need to play with a magician who knows the magic trick.

1 Pick any two-digit number, multiply it by 10, and write down the result. (For example, if you pick 34, write down 340.)

2 Now pick any one-digit number, multiply it by 9, and write that result down. (For example, if you pick 5, write down 45.)

3 Subtract the second number from the first number. (For the numbers in the example, you would find 340 − 45 = 295.)

4 Tell the magician this final number (295) and see if the magician can tell you your original two-digit number.

5 What is the magician doing? Why does this work?

Puzzle 3

1 Cut out the five cards from the sheet your teacher gives you.

2 Spread out the five cards face-up in front of you.

3 Choose a number from 1 to 31. Then, pick out all the cards that contain this same number.

4 Give the set of cards that have your number on them to the magician. The magician will find your number!

5 See if you can figure out the magic trick.

Big Ideas for Growing Mathematicians, 2007 © Zephyr Press

Magic Puzzles Continued

1	3	5	7
9	11	13	15
17	19	21	23
25	27	29	31

2	3	6	7
10	11	14	15
18	19	22	23
26	27	30	31

4	5	6	7
12	13	14	15
20	21	22	23
28	29	30	31

8	9	10	11
12	13	14	15
24	25	26	27
28	29	30	31

16	17	18	19
20	21	22	23
24	25	26	27
28	29	30	31

Big Ideas for Growing Mathematicians, 2007 © Zephyr Press

Cooperative Problems 3

The BIG Idea

Working together in math can help us see all sides of the problem.

Content Areas in This Activity
✔ Spatial reasoning
✔ Geometric terms such as *edge* and *face*

Process Skills Used in This Activity
✔ Creativity
✔ Reasoning
✔ Collaborative problem solving

Prerequisite Knowledge and Skills
✔ None

Age Appropriateness

This activity is appropriate for all ages as long as children can read simple clue cards.

The Mathematical Idea

Working on mathematical problem-solving tasks in small groups takes a bit of practice and requires cooperative skills. Although working mathematicians often solve problems by talking about them with colleagues, sometimes children are asked to work on mathematics problems alone, which fails to get them used to working effectively with others. The activities in this chapter help reacquaint children with the skills they need to share their ideas and work collaboratively, and they remind us explicitly that sometimes everyone's input is needed to solve a problem.

Here is a story that might motivate this activity. An old man approaches a boy in a grocery store. He asks the boy, "Do you have a minute?" The boy assumes he wants help, but instead the old man asks him a question. "How many sides do you see?" asks the old man, holding a box up in front of the boy's face.

"I see one," says the boy.

The old man moves back and again holds up the box. "Now how many?"

"Now I see three sides," says the boy.

The old man puts the box on its edge on a shopping cart and asks the boy to step back from it. The old man stands back from the box on the other side. He says to the boy "Now the two of us working together can see all six sides."*

Making It Work

Objectives

Students learn to work effectively together on spatial reasoning tasks by sharing their individual pieces of information about a shape's characteristics.

Materials

(for each group of three to four children)

Activity 1

✔ 2 yellow cubes
✔ 1 blue cube
✔ 1 red cube
✔ set of Activity 1 clue cards (see page 13)
✔ ziplock bag

Activity 2

✔ 2 yellow cubes
✔ 2 red cubes
✔ 1 green cube
✔ set of Activity 2 clue cards (see page 13–14)
✔ ziplock bag

Activity 3

✔ 2 red cubes
✔ 2 green cubes
✔ 1 yellow cube
✔ 1 blue cube
✔ set of Activity 3 clue cards (see page 14)
✔ ziplock bag

Note: *Cube colors may be changed but must be changed correspondingly on the clue cards!*

Preparation

Place one set of the required cubes and one set of clue cards (individually cut out from Activity Sheet) in an

---

*This story was told to me by Leisa Desmoulins. It originally appeared in the article "Towards a Redefinition of American Indian/ Alaska Native Education," *Canadian Journal of Native Education*, Vol. 20, No. 2.

HELPFUL TERMS

Face: the flat (two-dimensional) shape that makes up the outside surface of some three-dimensional objects, such as cubes or rectangular prisms

Edge: the (one-dimensional) line at which two faces of a shape meet

individual bag, such as a small ziplock bag, for each group of four students.

Procedure

1. Students work in groups of three or four. Each group should receive one prepared bag of materials.

2. Within each group, students should distribute the clue cards reasonably equally. Depending on the activity and the group size, they may get one, two, or three cards each. (Not everyone will have the same number of cards. The adult may choose to give out the cards if control is desired over who gets more cards due to reading level.)

3. Place the cubes in the center of the group so everyone can reach them.

4. One at a time, moving in a clockwise direction, each group member should read his or her clue card aloud, then move the blocks to reflect that card's clue, if possible.

5. Students continue reading their cards and moving the blocks until one shape has been created that satisfies the clues on every single clue card without changing the shape each time. Some students will have to reread their cards aloud and move the blocks again. The information on *all* the clue cards is required for a correct shape.

Suggestions

■ Sometimes children need to be reminded to double-check that the final shape satisfies all the cards.

■ One typical stumbling block is to forget that the cubes can also be stacked. After a suitable interval, a question such as "Is there any other way to arrange the cubes?" may prompt further thinking.

Assessment

The group has been successful when everyone has participated and the shape has satisfied all the clue cards. The group members are ready to move on to the next activity.

EXTENSION ACTIVITIES

Challenge the groups to create their own shape puzzle and clue cards. They should then test the activity they have created to be sure the cards are sufficient to build a unique shape. Groups can then exchange puzzles to solve.

Cooperative Problems Activity Sheet

In each of these activities, you will work with a group of three or four students. You will need a bag of materials for each activity.

1 Open the bag and place the cubes so everyone can reach them.

2 Hand out the clue cards. Not everyone needs to have the same number. For example, if there are six cards in the bag and there are four people in your group, some people will get two cards and some will get only one.

3 Starting with one person, read aloud the information on the card. Move the blocks to reflect what the clue card says.

4 One by one, moving in a clockwise direction, read your cards aloud. Work together to build a shape that satisfies all of the clues. Everyone can share their ideas about how the cubes should be placed.

5 When you move some of the blocks, leave the results in the middle so everyone can still see the shape.

6 When your group thinks it has the solution, test all of the clues to be sure the shape fits them all.

7 The group is finished when it has found a shape that satisfies all the clues.

8 When your group has successfully built all the shapes, try to create your own collaborative puzzle!

ACTIVITY 1	**Clue 1** **You can see all sides of the blue cube except the bottom.**
ACTIVITY 1	**Clue 2** **The blue cube touches the red cube on exactly 1 face.**
ACTIVITY 1	**Clue 3** **Each yellow cube touches the red cube on exactly 1 face.**
ACTIVITY 1	**Clue 4** **You can see only 2 faces of the red cube.**

ACTIVITY 2	**Clue 1** **You can see exactly 3 faces of each yellow cube.**
ACTIVITY 2	**Clue 2** **You can see all faces of each red cube except the bottom.**

Big Ideas for Growing Mathematicians, 2007 © Zephyr Press

Cooperative Problems Continued

ACTIVITY 2	**Clue 3** The yellow cubes do not touch each other anywhere, not even on an edge.
ACTIVITY 2	**Clue 4** The red cubes touch the yellow cubes on exactly 1 face each.
ACTIVITY 2	**Clue 5** You can see 3 faces of the green cube.
ACTIVITY 2	**Clue 6** The green cube touches each yellow cube on 1 face.

ACTIVITY 3	**Clue 1** The yellow cube and the blue cube touch on exactly 1 face.
ACTIVITY 3	**Clue 2** The 2 green cubes do not touch each other anywhere.

ACTIVITY 3	**Clue 3** Each red cube touches another cube on only 1 face.
ACTIVITY 3	**Clue 4** The blue cube touches each red cube along an edge.
ACTIVITY 3	**Clue 5** The blue cube touches each green cube along an edge.
ACTIVITY 3	**Clue 6** Each green cube touches 1 face of the yellow cube.
ACTIVITY 3	**Clue 7** Only 1 face of the yellow cube is not touching another cube.
ACTIVITY 3	**Clue 8** The 2 red cubes are not touching each other anywhere.

Big Ideas for Growing Mathematicians, 2007 © Zephyr Press

Lots of Dots

The BIG Idea

Students must work together effectively to solve this problem. That's an important skill in mathematics.

Content Areas in This Activity

✔ Spatial reasoning
✔ Terms such as *row, column, rectangle,* etc.

Process Skills Used in This Activity

✔ Communication
✔ Reasoning

Prerequisite Knowledge and Skills

✔ None

Age Appropriateness

This activity is appropriate for all ages.

The Mathematical Idea

As we saw in the tasks in chapter 3, "Cooperative Problems," children need to develop skills to share their ideas and work collaboratively, and sometimes everyone's input is needed to solve a problem.

This activity builds on the tasks in chapter 3. However, students must now communicate their reasoning by using words, rather than by moving blocks. This can be challenging at the beginning. They must also make decisions about which pieces of information can be assumed and which are crucial to describe. This is very like the work of a mathematician in that they are deciding which aspects of a problem to attend to and which to assume.

> **HELPFUL TERMS**
>
> **Row:** one horizontal set of spaces or cells, or in this case, dots
>
> **Column:** one vertical set of cells or dots

Making It Work

Objectives

Students learn to communicate their visualization and reasoning verbally so that others can understand. They also learn to follow others' descriptions and pose effective questions for clarification.

Materials

(for each group of four)

✔ full set of 24 cards (see page 19–22), copied onto card stock and cut out for each group of students

Preparation

One player shuffles the set of cards, leaving them face down.

Procedure

1. Students work in groups of four. They are not to look at each other's cards at any point, nor are they allowed to draw anything on paper.

2. The dealer passes out cards face down, one at a time, moving in a clockwise direction, to each group member in turn. Not all group members will receive the same number of cards.

3. Players should hold their own cards with the word "Top" printed on each card at the top.

4. The goal of the game is for each group to identify the one card that has no other copies. Starting with the player on the dealer's left, each player should describe one card in his or her hand. Other players look for this card in their own hand. Players can set their own identified duplicates in front of them.

5. Going clockwise, each player in turn should describe a remaining card. If the player has no cards left, the turn

---

EXTENSION ACTIVITIES

You can make the task more challenging by adding additional "duplicates" to the deck, making several sets of three using the templates already provided. Players should then describe the cards in their hands and put the sets together accordingly. Some groups will realize that "duplicates" may mean more than a pair and some will assume all cards are in pairs. (You may or may not decide to mention that there may be more than two of some cards.)

For another extension, challenge groups to create their own set of cards for a new game, then exchange decks with other groups to play a new round of games.

passes to the next player until only one player has a card left, or no matches can be made. That card is placed face up in the center.

6. Players should turn up each of their cards, checking to see that each card has a duplicate, until all cards are revealed. If all the other cards have a match, the center card should be the one without any other copies. Was the group correct?

Suggestions

The game can be adapted for use by very young or less verbal children by removing some of the sets of duplicate cards before handing them out.

Assessment

The group has been successful if they are able to identify the unique card.

Lots of Dots Activity Sheet

You will be working in groups of about four. Your task is to work in your group with the set of cards provided to identify the one card that is different from all the rest. But you have to do this without looking at each other's cards!

Method

Choose a group member as the dealer, who then hands out the cards face down around the group, clockwise, until they have all been given out. (There will be about five cards for each player, depending on the group size, but not everyone needs the same number.)

Each player should then look at his or her cards, arranging them with "Top" at the top.

Starting with the player at the dealer's left, take turns describing a card in your hand using only words. You may not show or draw what is on the card you are describing. Use clear words that others will understand. You *can* ask each other questions. The goal is to describe each card clearly enough that anyone else with that same card will be able to identify it. When you have finished describing the card, other players can set any cards they believe are a match aside in front of them.

Play continues clockwise, one player at a time, until only one card is held in a player's hand. If there is more than one card left, and nobody can make a match, somebody has made an error. In that case, you may replay this hand, with everyone starting from their original hand, or place all cards face down in the center, shuffle, and start over!

If only one card remains, place that card face *up* in the center of the table. Then, turn up all face-down cards to see if any of the other cards match the center card. The center card should be the one card without any other copies. Was your group correct?

Big Ideas for Growing Mathematicians, 2007 © Zephyr Press

Lots of Dots Continued

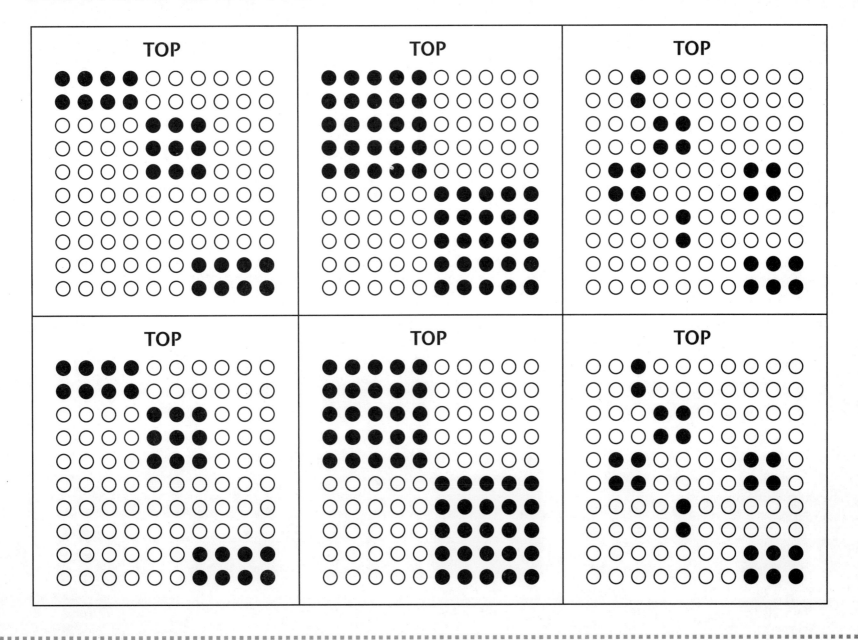

Lots of Dots Continued

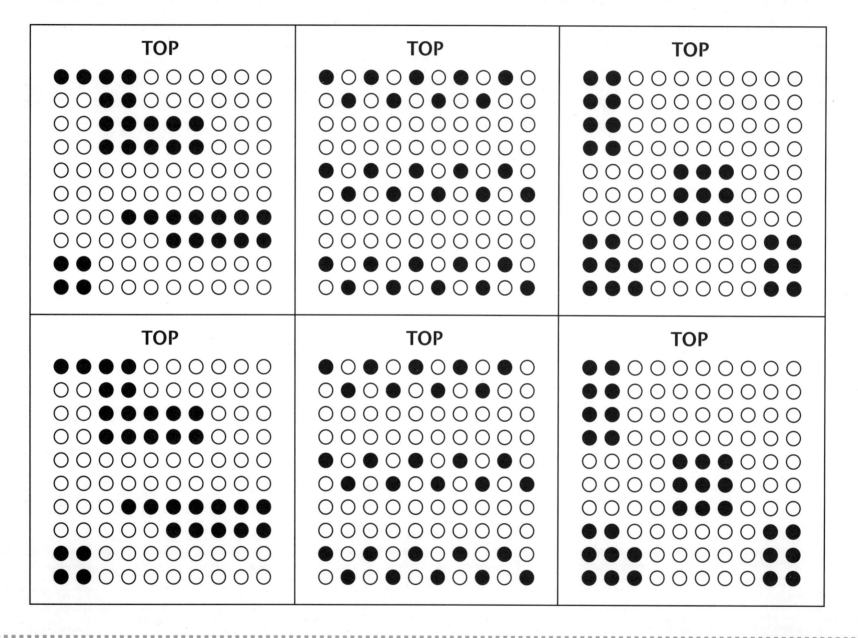

Big Ideas for Growing Mathematicians, 2007 © Zephyr Press

Lots of Dots Continued

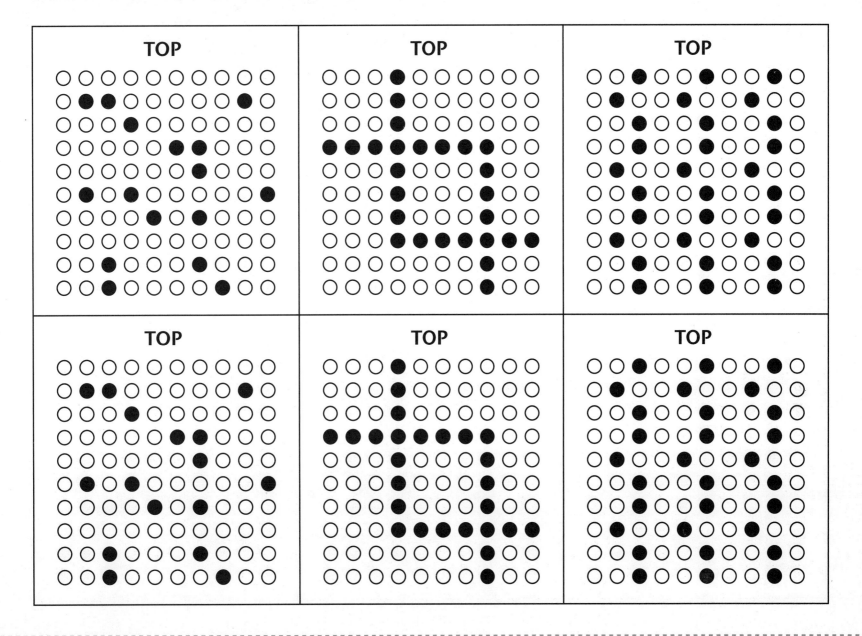

Lots of Dots Continued

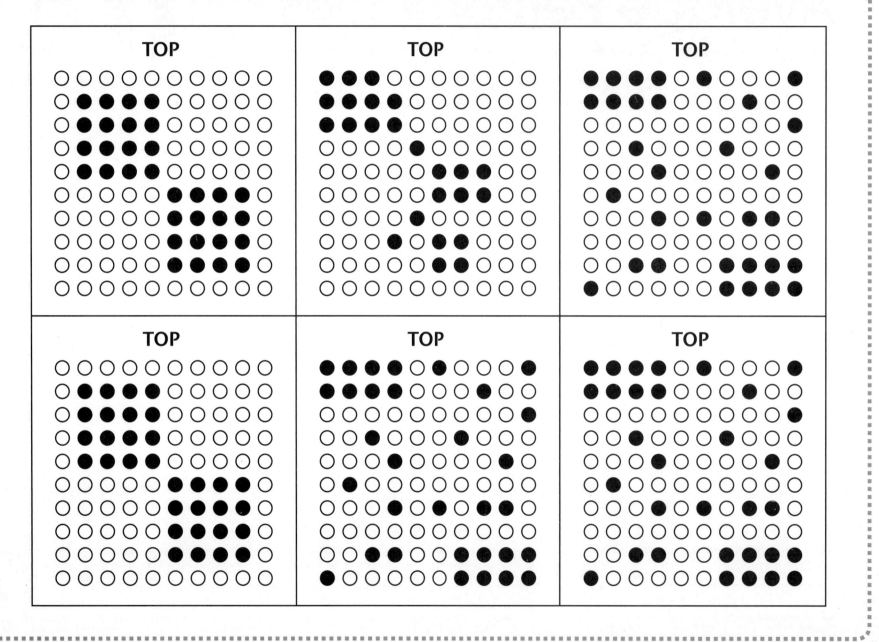

Average Pentominoes

5

The BIG Idea

The average, or mean, amount is what everyone would get if we shared a quantity equally.

Content Areas in This Activity

✔ Numeracy
✔ Number sense
✔ Hundreds charts
✔ Patterning
✔ Mean value
✔ Spatial reasoning
✔ Pentominoes

Process Skills Used in This Activity

✔ Problem solving
✔ Reasoning

Prerequisite Knowledge and Skills

✔ Calculating the average of two-digit numbers

Age Appropriateness

Children who are able to add two-digit numbers and divide (possibly with a calculator) will be able to do this activity.

The Mathematical Idea

The mean or average of several numbers is often introduced only by a definition of how to calculate it. In fact, the mean amount is an equal share. For example, if we took all the wealth in the country and shared it equally, everyone would have the same income; this number would be the mean.

In this activity, children get a sense of this notion using the patterns in the hundreds chart. If they use a symmetric pentomino, it will be possible to place the piece so the middle spot is the mean value, and the other numbers to the left and right (or up and down) balance each other. If the pentomino is not symmetric, this will be impossible. For example, a one-by-five pentomino placed horizontally covering 44, 45, 46, 47, and 48 will have a mean value for the five squares of 46. You can see this is true if you imagine moving one unit from the 47 and giving it to the 45. Now both these two numbers (45 and 47) are 46. Similarly, we move two from 48 and give it to 44. Now all five values would be 46. This will also be true if the pentomino is placed vertically, to cover 26, 36, 46, 56, and 66, except we are moving tens instead of units. Other symmetric pieces could also share this outcome.

Making It Work

Objectives

Children are reminded of the predictable patterns of numbers in the hundreds chart. They will think about possible pentomino layouts, including the notion of symmetry. Finally, they investigate the idea of average or mean as an equal share.

HELPFUL TERMS

Average, or (more formally) mean: the calculation whereby you add all the numbers in a list and divide by how many there are

Pentomino: a shape made from five squares touching on at least one edge

Symmetry: the idea of something being the same on both sides of a mirror line, that is, an image is reflected in the line

---

Materials

✔ hundreds chart for each student or student pair (see page 26)

✔ either a blank hundreds chart of the same size to create pentominoes or pentomino templates already to cut out with squares of the same size as the squares in the hundreds chart; several per person (see page 27)

Preparation

Copy the activity sheets and give one set to each student.

Procedure

1. Give each student or pair of students a hundreds chart and several pentominoes. Make sure that each has a mixture of symmetric and nonsymmetric pentominoes. (Students can use ones already drawn (page 27), or cut out their own from a blank grid (page 27).

2. Tell student teams to pick a number on the hundreds chart somewhere near the middle. (That is, avoid the top and bottom rows, 1 through 10 and 91 through 100, and the left and right columns.) There needs to be space around each number so it shouldn't be on an edge of the chart. For example, teams might pick 37, 53, or 46.

3. Now ask students to place each pentomino over the chosen number and four others, so that the average of the five numbers covered is the initial number chosen. Which pentominoes work? Why?

4. Have participants try another number to draw general conclusions about the shape of the pentominoes and the relationship to finding the mean value.

Suggestions

Encourage students to explore an easier way to figure out if a piece will fit in a certain place. Do they really have to average all five numbers beneath the pentomino to determine if they have the piece located properly? What is the averaging calculation actually doing?

Assessment

Students could be given another pentomino and asked if it can be placed on the hundreds chart so the average is a certain number. They can explain their reasons for predicting whether this would be possible or not.

EXTENSION ACTIVITIES

You might ask students to create pentominoes of different shapes from the ones they already chose and to predict which ones will work and which will not.

A more challenging idea would be to work with a different chart pattern; for example, use a chart of even numbers (the "two times" table), or multiples of five, and do the same activity.

Another related activity would be to give students five bags of pennies, with different numbers or pennies in each bag (or one or more bags with the same number). Ask them to show with the pennies how they would find the average. This could be done by putting the same number in each bag. To avoid discussions about cutting pennies into pieces, make sure the total number of pennies is a multiple of five. For example, fill the five bags initially randomly with a total of 25, 30, 35, or 40 pennies.

Average Pentominoes Activity Sheet

In this activity you will be using pentominoes your teacher gives you and the hundreds chart to the right to investigate the idea of an average.

1 Select a number on the chart near the middle.

2 Work with each pentomino separately to see if you can place it on the hundreds chart so that the average value, or mean value, of the five numbers it covers is the number you've chosen, and that the number you've chosen is under the pentomino.

3 If you can find a spot that works, can you find another spot?

4 After trying this activity with all the pentominoes, see if you can draw a conclusion about which pieces work and which do not. Test your theory with other numbers.

1	2	3	4	5	6	7	8	9	10
11	12	13	14	15	16	17	18	19	20
21	22	23	24	25	26	27	28	29	30
31	32	33	34	35	36	37	38	39	40
41	42	43	44	45	46	47	48	49	50
51	52	53	54	55	56	57	58	59	60
61	62	63	64	65	66	67	68	69	70
71	72	73	74	75	76	77	78	79	80
81	82	83	84	85	86	87	88	89	90
91	92	93	94	95	96	97	98	99	100

Big Ideas for Growing Mathematicians, 2007 © Zephyr Press

Average Pentominoes Continued

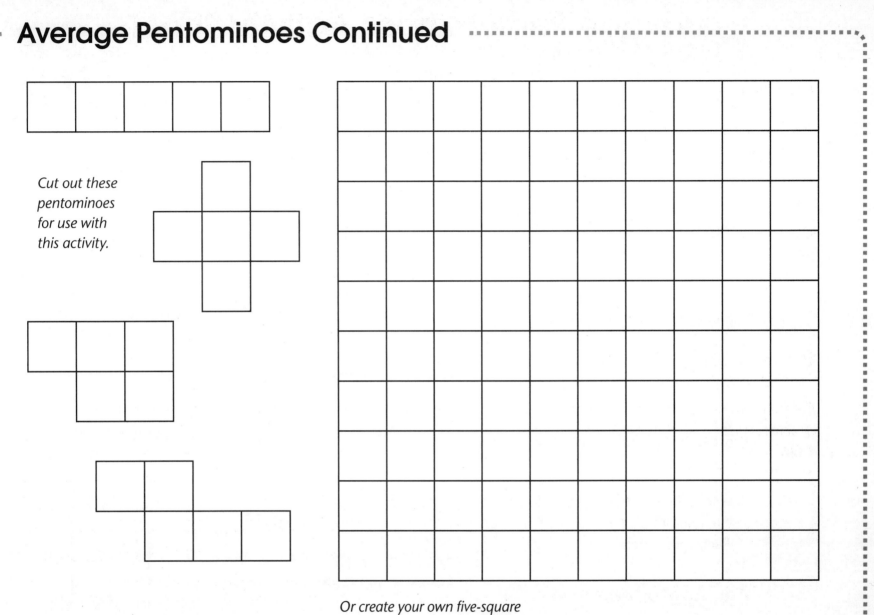

Cut out these pentominoes for use with this activity.

Or create your own five-square pentominoes using the blank grid.

Distributing Tiles

The BIG Idea

Most rules of algebra are based on geometry.

Content Areas in This Activity

✔ Rectangular area
✔ Multiplication models
✔ Distributive property
✔ Basic rules of algebra

Process Skills Used in This Activity

✔ Reasoning

Prerequisite Knowledge and Skills

✔ Multiplication
✔ Rectangular area

Age Appropriateness

This activity is appropriate for all ages.

The Mathematical Idea

Algebra is sometimes taught as if it is simply a series of rules that don't have any meaning in and of themselves. In fact, these rules are generally a type of mathematical shortcut for processes that have geometric meaning.

For example, students learn to expand expressions in high school with an unknown such as n, but they often (incorrectly) write things like $3 \times (n + 2) = 3n + 2$, rather than $3 \times (n + 2) = 3n + 6$. This sometimes happens because students are unable to picture what that parenthetical expression means. For example, let's let $n = 4$ in the expression given and draw a picture to represent $3 \times (4 + 2)$, which is the value of the expression

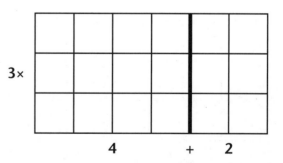

using 4 for n. The 4 + 2 is shown as the **width** of the bottom of the picture on page 28. The entire expression is multiplied by 3, which is the **height** of the rectangle.

From the picture, it's clear that we have to multiply *both* numbers on the bottom row by the 3. So 3 × (4 + 2) equals 3 × (6), or 18, as well as equaling (3 × 4) + (3 × 2) = 12 + 6 = 18. This rule or generalization is known as the *distributive property of multiplication over addition.*

The same property applies to more complicated expressions. For example, there are similar rules for expanding things like (n + 3) × (n + 2). Again, let n be 4, and draw a picture to investigate.

From the picture, you can see that (4 + 3) × (4 + 2) is 16 + 8 + 12 + 6. Remember that the *n* could have

been any number. If n was 6, the upper left block would be 6 by 6, and the upper right block would have a height of 6, while the lower left block would have a width of 6. The other dimensions are constant (3 by 2), so the lower right block doesn't change in area.

There is also a procedural rule children are sometimes taught to do this expanding, which tells them how to multiply each pair of numbers. This rule makes sense when we see the picture. Sometimes the acronym FOIL (**f**irst, **o**utside, **i**nside, **l**ast) is used to help students remember the four multiplication steps. A picture is much easier. (You won't find the term *FOIL* in the glossary of this book! You don't need it when you understand the *idea*.)

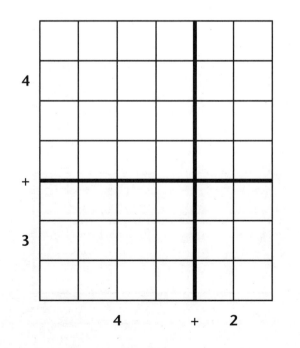

4

+

3

4   +   2

Making It Work

....

Objectives

Students investigate the rules of algebra using tiles to represent whole numbers.

┌─────────────── **HELPFUL TERMS** ───────────────┐

Binomial: an expression with two terms in it, such as n + 2

└───┘

Materials

✔ 1-centimeter-square tiles, or any square tiles; these can be cut out of heavy paper from grid paper if tiles are not available

Preparation

Prepare the tiles in advance, about 50 for each pair or small group of students.

Procedure

1. Have students investigate the expressions shown on the activity sheet, or other similar expressions provided.

2. Encourage groups to come up with other ways of writing the expressions and eventually to generalize their findings.

Suggestions

The speed of progression of the tasks can be modified based on students' level of preparation and grade level.

Assessment

Students should be able to model other similar expressions and state several forms of writing them after these activities.

EXTENSION ACTIVITIES

Some students may be ready by seventh or eighth grade (or even sooner, depending on the student) to begin to think about an unknown length, perhaps called n or x. Given an unknown-length tile (use another color and be sure to emphasize this tile is like an imaginary elastic—it can be any length so we can't measure it), as well as a square x by x tile (x squared), can we create generalizations for the rules discovered with numbers?

For example, $(x + 2)(x + 3)$ is shown below to equal $x^2 + 3x + 2x + 6$ or $x^2 + 5x + 6$.

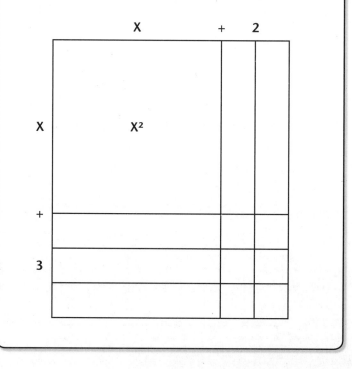

Distributing Tiles Activity Sheet

For this activity you will be working with a partner, and you will need some square tiles. Each of these square tiles represents 1.

Part A

1 Build a 3 × 4 rectangle with the tiles and find its area. The area is the number of tiles in the rectangle.

2 Now calculate 3 × 4. The answer should be the same as your rectangle's area. So the area is a model of 3 × 4.

3 Model 2 × 5 using the same method of building a rectangle. The rectangle is nice to use because it's easy to see that 2 × 5 and 5 × 2 have the same picture—but it's turned on its side.

4 Now model 4 + 2. Let's show it like this:

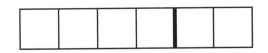

5 Can you model 3 × (4 + 2)? Make a rectangle of 3 rows to model the "3 times" part of the expression.

6 One way to calculate 3 × (4 + 2) is to find 3 × 6. Using your picture, can you think of another way to calculate the total area using separate sections?

7 Which way would be easier to use to answer 5 × (8 + 10)?

8 Practice with your tiles. Build a model and find the answer by calculating the area more than one way:

a. 2 × (1 + 9)   **b.** 4 × (3 + 5)

Part B

1 Calculate the answer to (4 + 3) × (4 + 2) by adding the numbers in the brackets first, and then multiplying.

2 Using your rectangle model, build a rectangle to show the multiplication. (Hint: Try making your rectangle 4 + 3 or 7 units high and 4 + 2 or 6 units wide.)

3 Is there another way you could think of to add up the area in your rectangle? The sections in this picture might help you:

Big Ideas for Growing Mathematicians, 2007 © Zephyr Press

Distributing Tiles Continued

4 From the picture, you can see that (4 + 3) × (4 + 2) is 16 + 8 + 12 + 6. Where do the numbers 16, 8, 12, and 6 come from? In other words, can you find a rule for *another* way to calculate (4 + 3) × (4 + 2) other than by calculating 7 × 6?

5 Practice by showing 5 × (2 + 6) with the tiles. Find the answer two ways using your tiles.

6 Can you write a general statement or description to help you remember what you learned in this activity?

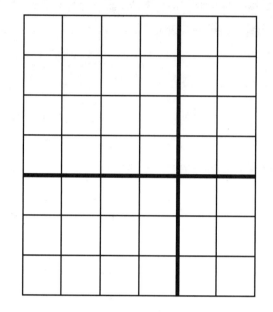

Big Ideas for Growing Mathematicians, 2007 © Zephyr Press

Guess My Rule

7

The BIG Idea

Predicting a number from a related one is something math does very well.

Content Areas in This Activity
✔ Patterning
✔ Numeracy

Process Skills Used in This Activity
✔ Reasoning

Prerequisite Knowledge and Skills
✔ Multiplication
✔ Applying formulas/pattern rules

Age Appropriateness

This activity can be adapted for many ages.

The Mathematical Idea

Mathematics is very good at describing numeric patterns. It has even been described as the science of patterns. Recognizing and finding expressions for these patterns is thus an important skill.

Sometimes it is possible that different people will be able to find relationships in different ways and that more than one way of seeing a pattern is possible. Different-looking rules that give the same result are called *equivalent*. Using algebra you can show them to be the same. Working together allows for different perspectives and shared thinking—and it makes the process just so much more engaging for kids!

HELPFUL TERMS

Frame number or input number: both are ways of identifying a starting number, which a rule, pattern, or relationship changes into a result, answer, or output value

Function: a mathematical name for a pattern rule that relates one number to a resultant number

---

Making It Work

Objectives

Students investigate creating and finding pattern rules.

Materials

✔ a "magic" box (One large enough for a child to go inside is fun for smaller children; I have also used a table covered with a sheet. Older children may enjoy having the magician wear a magic hat.)

✔ several dozen 1-centimeter cubes or pennies to be used for counters

Preparation

None

Procedure

This activity works with children in small groups of three to six, or large (whole-class) groups. For younger children, and children trying this activity for the first time, concrete materials are useful. Later, numbers can be relayed verbally.

1. Select one child to be the magician. The magician is the only person who knows the magic rule (which may have been supplied by an adult).

2. If hands-on materials are used, such as cubes or pennies, select an "input" person to hand the magician the materials.

3. The participants have the task of determining the magic rule. Either the input person should hand a certain number of cubes or pennies to the magician, based on the participants' directions. If manipulatives are not used, a group member should tell the magician a number.

4. The magician should then perform the magic rule on the number given and hand (or write) the resultant number of cubes or pennies back to the input person as output.

5. It's helpful to use a student recorder to write down the inputs and outputs on chart paper or a blackboard.

6. The participants continue to offer numbers and receive answers from the magician, until someone thinks he or she can guess the rule. If the guess is incorrect, play continues.

7. If the participant guesses the rule correctly, he or she becomes the next magician and is given a new magic rule to use.

Suggestions

It's helpful to have an adult on hand who also knows the magic rule; he or she should check to make sure the magician doesn't make a calculation error. This type of error can make the game very confusing for participants . . . if not impossible! Participants can also be guided in good choices of input values—choosing the right numbers to try is in itself an important skill.

The adult should initially choose the rules so as to control the difficulty level. Care should be taken to use rules that generate positive results if concrete materials are used and if children haven't used integers. For example, the rule "Subtract 5 from the input number" is problematic with counters representing only positive numbers, should an input value less than 5 be given, but the rule "Double the number and add 1" is fine.

Beginning Rule Ideas:

- Double the number
- Add 4 to the number

Progressing to Two-Step Rules:

- Double the number and subtract 1
- Multiply the number by 3 and add 2

Challenging Rules:

- Multiply the number by itself
- Triple the number and subtract 2
- Multiply the number by itself and add 1

Assessment

I have found children make big improvements in their pattern-recognition skills using this activity. Eventually they will be able to tackle written lists, but sometimes they find these lists much less engaging. The best assessment would be to see how well everyone is able to do with finding a rule using the game, maybe writing down their answers individually, instead of asking the magician. But this activity is more about fluency than formal assessment.

EXTENSION ACTIVITIES

Children can be challenged to think up their own rules when they are the magician. This might allow for more challenging rules such as "The number squared plus 2."

Guess My Rule Activity Sheet

You will be playing this game in a group. You will take turns being the magician. Everyone else will be trying to figure out the magician's magic rule.

1 The teacher will tell the magician a magic rule.

2 You may use pennies or 1-centimeter cubes as counters to help you. Otherwise, participants will take turns calling out a number.

3 An input person should hand a small number of cubes to the magician. The magician will perform the magic rule and hand the cubes representing the result to an output person, who will then count the result.

4 Have a recorder write the input and output numbers on a chart to keep track of the results.

5 If a participant believes he or she knows the rule, the player should raise a hand and state it.

6 If the rule is correct, the player becomes the magician in the next round. If not, play continues.

Here's an example of how it might work:

An adult whispers the rule "Double the number" to the magician. Participants then suggest an input number of 2, and the input person hands the magician 2 cubes (or tells the magician, "Two").

The magician doubles this input number (without directly revealing the rule) and hands 4 cubes to the output person. He or she counts them and calls out, "Four!" The recorder writes "2" and "4" on the board in a chart form.

At this point, perhaps a participant thinks the rule might be "Add 2." The person calls out this guess to the magician, who replies, "No."

If you are a participant and think you know the rule, you may want to check your idea by trying a number that will verify that rule. With a bit of practice, you will get much better at finding the rules quickly.

Play continues with more input numbers until someone finds the correct rule.

Big Ideas for Growing Mathematicians, 2007 © Zephyr Press

The Rice Problem

8

The BIG Idea

When you keep on doubling a number, even a small number, amazing things happen!

Content Areas in This Activity

✔ Numeracy
✔ Estimation
✔ Measurement of weights
✔ Measurement conversion
✔ Patterning
✔ Exponential functions
✔ Scientific notation (depending on the calculator used)
✔ Nonlinear patterns

Process Skills Used in This Activity

✔ Problem solving
✔ Reasoning

Prerequisite Knowledge and Skills

✔ Multiplication
✔ Place value for large numbers

Age Appropriateness

This activity is appropriate for students who are able to work with large numbers and use calculators. An understanding of scientific notation is not a prerequisite but may emerge.

The Mathematical Idea

When we think of doubling something 30 times or so, we intuitively might think we would get a result about two times 30 times as big. In fact, we'd get a result 2^{30} times as big. That's 2×2 times as big—there are 30 twos in there! That's 1,073,741,824. I had to do that by hand by multiplying big powers of 2 because my calculator wouldn't give me all the digits! The calculator changed to something called *scientific notation,* a kind of shorthand for very big (or very small) numbers. When I typed in "2^{30}" it gave me 1.0737418 E09. On a different calculator it could also be shown as 1.0737418 10 9. In either case it means to take the number on the screen of

1.0737418 and multiply it by 10 nine times, or in other words 1.0737418 × 10 × 10 × 10 × 10 × 10 × 10 × 10 × 10 × 10. This results in moving the decimal point nine places to the right, which means adding two zeros. Of course as you do this you miss the last two digits that don't show on the calculator screen, the digits replaced by zeros, so you are really off by, in this case, 24 (the two digits farthest to the right). But that's not such a big deal for a number that is over a billion.

Rarely do you get a chance to really see what these kinds of numbers, called exponentials, are like. At a certain point, as long as the number you keep multiplying by is bigger than 1, they get humongous. (That's pretty scary when you realize that population growth is exponential.)

— HELPFUL TERMS —

Scientific notation: notation in which a big number is expressed with one number before the decimal place, called the base, raised to a power of 10 (The exponent on the 10 tells us how many times to multiply by 10 to get the actual value we are trying to represent. For example, 7,654,321 is 7.654321×10^6 in scientific notation.)

Exponential: a number written as a base number raised to an exponent (For example, 2^3 is an exponential that equals 8. If the exponent is an unknown or a *variable,* it is called an *exponential function*—for example, in the expression 2^x, where x can be any number.)

Making It Work

Objectives

Students gain firsthand knowledge about the effect of exponential functions, although naming them is not essential. Students also practice estimation, counting methods, and converting to appropriate units in a real problem-solving context.

Materials

✔ small bag of rice that has a label showing the weight of the contents
✔ measuring cup
✔ tablespoon or 16-milliliter measuring spoon

Preparation

Counting out and measuring or weighing 100 grains of rice in advance may save time, but it is not necessary. You might choose a different way to estimate the number of grains to make a certain weight. However, it's more fun to let kids figure out their own way to do it—in fact it's an important part of the thinking in this problem.

Procedure

This activity works best in small groups.

1. Hand the activity sheet out to participants or explain the problem to them verbally.

2. Ideally, materials should be available, but there's no need to provide a specific method—the determination of the method is in fact an important part of the mathematical learning.

Suggestions

It may help to remind participants that they are looking for an estimate of the weight, not an exact number.

To get started, it might be a good idea to make a chart of the number of grains for each day. An old calendar or hundreds chart (see page 26) would make a good chart. Ask participants to look for a pattern. If you know the number on a given day, how would you find the number for the next day?

It is possible to answer the problem using an exact number for each day and following the doubling pattern, with the final day being just over a billion grains of rice. This takes a while, of course. Or participants might determine a pattern rule; something like "double yesterday" or "double one fewer times than the day number"—e.g., for day 31, double the initial grain 30 times. (A more formal formula for the number of grains of rice on day 31 is 2^{30}, but students do not need to express it

this way now. They will learn this in high school.) This number is then converted to a weight. Final answers will vary because different types of rice will weigh different amounts; wild rice, for example, is much heavier than instant rice.

Assessment

The best assessment would be to have children be able to explain their thinking. Alternatively, children could work with a related problem with different numbers.

EXTENSION ACTIVITIES

Children could be encouraged to graph their results for the rice problem, with the number of days on the horizontal axis, and the weight or number of grains on the vertical axis. They could also predict (based on the graph) what might happen if the pattern continued.

Population growth is another important example of exponential growth. You might ask children to do some research on the Web on the population of the planet over the last 100 years and then graph this data. Have them discuss what this graph might be telling us.

The Rice Problem Activity Sheet

The queen of Mathvia has made an unusual request of one of her subjects whom she wishes to punish for bad behavior. The subject is to deliver rice to the palace each day for the month of January according to the following pattern. The first day, he is to deliver one grain of rice. The second day he is to bring two grains, the third day four grains, the fourth day eight grains, and so on. Each day the amount doubles.

Your job as assistant to the queen is to check that the correct amount has been delivered on the last day.

1 How many grains of rice should be delivered on day 31? You may wish to begin the problem by using an old calendar and writing out the number of grains for the first few days. Is there a pattern? How can you use the pattern to determine the number on January 31?

2 If you find it too difficult to count this many grains, determine a method to estimate the weight of the amount of rice on day 31, using the weight printed on a rice package to help you.

Big Ideas for Growing Mathematicians, 2007 © Zephyr Press

Lines, Squares, Cubes, and Hypercubes

9

The BIG Idea

We can imagine a cube from a two-dimensional (flat) picture. But can we image a four-dimensional "hypercube" from a three-dimensional model?

Content Areas in This Activity
✔ Spatial reasoning
✔ Terminology such as *edge* and *vertex*

Process Skills Used in This Activity
✔ Visualization

Prerequisite Knowledge and Skills
✔ None

Age Appropriateness

This activity is appropriate for all ages.

The Mathematical Idea

A line segment—we'll just use the word *line* for short—is a one-dimensional object. The only thing you can measure is its length. Theoretically it has no diameter or width. It's a bit hard to draw a line with absolutely no width, so you might pretend to do it by drawing a very thin line with a pencil and thinking of it as having no width. It works reasonably well to create a one-dimensional object—a line—on a two-dimensional medium, such as paper. We can also imagine a line in three-dimensional space by holding a thin, straight wire in the air, for example.

A square is a two-dimensional object. If you take four equal line segments (lines with a set length) and set them at right angles (90 degrees) in a plane to form a closed shape, you create a square. All the edges are perpendicular to the adjoining edges. Since a square is a two-dimensional object, you can draw it easily on two-dimensional paper, or model it by creating an outline to hold in the air in three-dimensional space. It would be hard to model a square in one-dimensional space, but one-dimensional space is hard for us to imagine anyway. Another way to think of creating a square by starting with a line is to move a copy of the line parallel to the original line along the page. If you slide the line the same distance away as the line is long, and join the ends of both lines with two more lines the same length, you form a square. Two of these lines meet at each vertex of the square.

Now it's time to think three dimensionally. You can create a model of a cube by joining 12 same-length line segments, one for each edge. Straws work fine for the edges as long as you pretend they have no diameter. All the edges meet at 90-degree angles.

You can model a cube in three dimensions, but we often like to draw a picture that represents a cube on paper. This is an image of a three-dimensional object drawn on a two-dimensional medium—a flat sheet of paper. You won't be able to show all the angles as 90 degrees. You have to sort of fake it by making a perspective drawing and *imagining* the third set of angles to be 90 degrees. Each vertex of a cube is the meeting point of three edges, whether it is built in three dimensions or

drawn on paper. The difference with a paper drawing is that you have to imagine each of the angles between the lines forming the edges to be 90 degrees at each vertex.

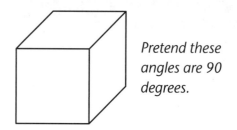

Pretend these angles are 90 degrees.

Another way to think of getting a cube from a square is to imagine sliding a square in the perpendicular direction and then joining the vertices.

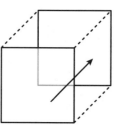

Extending the idea of what you can do to show a three-dimensional cube on two-dimensional paper, you can create an image of a four-dimensional cube, called a hypercube, in three-dimensional space. It isn't a *real* hypercube of course—just a visual image of it, like the picture of the cube you draw on paper. You have to imagine the fourth dimension because you are short a dimension using three-dimensional space. All sets of

---

HELPFUL TERMS

Edge: a straight line that bounds a closed shape

Vertex: point at which two or more edges meet

edges should really meet the others at 90 degrees, but like the cube drawn on paper, you have to imagine the last set of edges meeting the others at right angles. There will now be four edges meeting at each vertex.

You can use similar reasoning to how we slid a square to form a cube. Start with a cube. Now slide the cube in a perpendicular fourth direction—OK, you need a little imagination here—and join all the vertices. The two cubes and joining lines have 32 edges, so you'd better have 32 straws on hand to build the model!

To learn more, try a Web search using the keywords *spinning hypercubes*. (Kids can do this, too.) You'll be amazed!

Making It Work

Objectives

Students gain experience with multidimensional representation and visualization.

Materials

Various materials will work—for example:
- ✔ straws
- ✔ pipe cleaners
- ✔ glue sticks
- ✔ tape

Preparation

None

Procedure

1. Guide participants to create a square from four straws joined at the ends by a length of pipe cleaner that has been folded in half and inserted.

2. Use a glue stick on the pipe cleaner to help hold it in place, and tape it until the glue dries.

3. Participants can discuss various aspects of the square. For example, it is a two-dimensional shape, and all the enclosed angles are 90 degrees.

4. Have students draw their models, which will also be two dimensional. Each vertex (corner) of the square has two edges meeting at 90 degrees.

5. Now create a cube. One way for them to think of creating a cube is to first create a second square. Place one square on the table on top of the other, then raise up the top square parallel to the table, lifting it up by the length of one side.

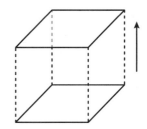

6. Join the new vertices with four vertical straws. There will now be 12 edges and 8 vertices. At each vertex three edges meet at 90 degrees.

7. You have modeled the cube in three dimensions, but to draw it on paper you have to use perspective—that is, you have to imagine the last set of angles to be 90 degrees.

8. Now use the same method to create a model of a hypercube. Imagine moving another cube in a perpendicular direction, and joining the vertices. This would make four edges meet at each vertex, and all four angles would be 90 degrees. But you have to imagine the fourth set is 90 degrees; your model in three dimensions is similar to a perspective drawing. The arrow below shows the direction of the slide of the cube.

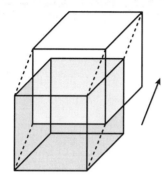

9. Now join all vertices of the top and bottom cubes. The arrow is the first of these new edges. Four edges must meet at each vertex.

Suggestions

As more edges (or straws) get joined, it will be harder to insert more pipe cleaners into the existing vertices. Tape may help secure the last straws.

Assessment

Students can discuss their increased understanding of the idea of dimension. No formal assessment is appropriate. If kids are excited or intrigued, the activity has been successful.

EXTENSION ACTIVITIES

Students might be challenged to count the number of vertices (16) and edges (32) in the hypercube. They could also check out some Internet sites using the keywords *spinning hypercubes* to see animations. Some are excellent!

Students might also be challenged to write a story about what a two-dimensional person might see in our three-dimensional world. For example, if you could only see the floor of your classroom, what might you see happening?

Lines, Squares, Cubes, and Hypercubes
Activity Sheet

In this activity you will investigate the relationship between one-, two-, three-, and even four-dimensional objects. Building simple objects will help you visualize them.

1 Start with one dimension. It wouldn't be all that exciting living in a one-dimensional world. This line is a picture of a one-dimensional object.

This line can only change length, its only dimension. Theoretically, it doesn't have any width. Of course the picture of a line really does have a tiny width, but you have to imagine it has no width at all. If you are using straws to model a line, you have to pretend the straw has no diameter or width—it just has a length.

2 Now create a square by placing one straw right next to another and moving one of them in another direction, as shown:

3 Finish the square by adding the other two top and bottom edges. This may seem a silly way to think of making a square right now, but it will help your thinking when you get to four dimensions.

4 Using this idea, add a straw to the top and bottom of your model and attach the corners (vertices) together to form a square. You can use a piece of pipe cleaner with glue on it inserted in each straw. Use tape to help hold the join until the glue dries.

5 Now move to three dimensions and create a cube. Draw a picture of a cube on your paper (like the one shown here) by pretending the lines that go in the third dimension are 90 degrees. You have to draw them in perspective because you don't really have the third dimension to work in.

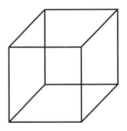

6 Now make a real cube with straws. First, make a second square and place it on top of the first one, with both sitting flat on the tabletop. Lift up the top square keeping it parallel to the tabletop, then join each vertex to the one below it with a new straw. Sliding the square upward into the third dimension creates the cube. Each vertex of our three-dimensional cube has three edges (straws) joining. (What do you think will happen in four dimensions?)

Big Ideas for Growing Mathematicians, 2007 © Zephyr Press

Lines, Squares, Cubes, and Hypercubes Continued

7 Now it's time to make a three-dimensional model of a four-dimensional cube called a hypercube. Four straws (edges) will meet at each vertex and they will all be at 90 degrees to one another—at least in four-dimensional space they will. In the normal three-dimensional world you will have to imagine the last angle to be 90 degrees to the others, just as you did with the picture of the cube on a flat, two-dimensional paper.

8 Use the same method to expand your model as before. First, make a second cube. Now imagine sliding one cube in a direction perpendicular to all the other directions (in the fourth dimension). Now join all the vertices with new straws. It will look like a cube within a cube. You will have to imagine all the angles at the last set of joins to be 90 degrees, and each vertex has four straws meeting. (You will probably have to use tape to join the last straws as the straws may be too full of pipe cleaner by now to add more inside the straw.)

9 The picture below shows the second cube slid into the fourth dimension shown by the arrow. The arrow shows one of the new edges. There are seven more vertices to join to create the hypercube. Can you imagine it?

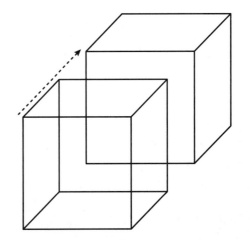

Big Ideas for Growing Mathematicians, 2007 © Zephyr Press

Fractional Salaries

The BIG Idea

Different models of division are useful for understanding fractions.

Content Areas in This Activity
✔ Fractions
✔ Division

Process Skills Used in This Activity
✔ Problem solving
✔ Reasoning

Prerequisite Knowledge and Skills
✔ Multiplication
✔ Fraction terminology

Age Appropriateness

This activity is appropriate for middle-school ages.

The Mathematical Idea

When most people think of division, they think of splitting or dividing up a number into groups. Some people are surprised to learn there are other models of division that are very useful, especially when working with fractions. Another way to think of division is by measuring the number of groups, or counting amounts of a certain size. For example, the question "How many costumes can we make from 10 yards of fabric, if each costume needs 2 yards?" is a question using the measurement idea or model. This model is helpful for understanding division of fractions.

You could also interpret a problem such as $3 \div \frac{1}{2}$ as "How many $\frac{1}{2}$s fit in 3?" It is then easy to relate this to "How many vests can we make from 3 yards of material if each vest needs $\frac{1}{2}$ yard of material?" As there are two vests possible per yard, the answer is 3 yards × 2 vests per yard, or 6 vests. (Did you notice that to divide by $\frac{1}{2}$ we actually ended up multiplying by 2? Sound familiar?)

This activity uses a social-justice theme to introduce the measurement model of division, which is particularly useful for dividing fractions.

Making It Work

Objectives

Students gain conceptual understanding of what is happening when we divide by a fraction.

Materials

✔ calculators (optional)

Preparation

None

Procedure

1. It might be helpful to begin the lesson by discussing examples of division that use a measurement model. For example, a question similar to "If we have 2 pounds of tofu, how many ¼-pound sandwiches can we make?" might form a good introduction to this idea of division. Examples with measurement of fabric or ribbon are also useful as the materials are easy to find or draw.

2. From there, students should be encouraged to work on the activity sheet, possibly in pairs or small groups.

3. After finishing the activity, it might be worthwhile to discuss how well these ideas generalize. For example, in the sandwich example above, you see there are four sandwiches possible per pound of tofu, so the number

> ### HELPFUL TERMS
>
> **Measurement model for division:** a model in which division is understood as measuring how many of the divisor amount fit into the dividend. So you can think of 3 ÷ ½ as measuring or counting how many ½s there are in 3.

of possible sandwiches is 2 × 4. In fact, it is always true that when you divide by a unit fraction, you can multiply the amount you have by how many of the fraction fit into a whole. So 2 ÷ ¼ = 2 × 4.

4. Dividing by a nonunit fraction follows easily. When you divide by a number you can do it in stages. For example, 100 ÷ 20 is the same as 100 ÷ 10 ÷ 2 = (100 ÷ 10) ÷ 2 = 10 ÷ 2 = 5. (Try it!) So, for example, 6 ÷ ¾ is the same as (6 ÷ 3) ÷ ¼ = 2 ÷ ¼ = 2 × 4 = 8.

Suggestions

Students who have trouble working with the larger more realistic numbers in the activity may need examples with smaller numbers to get started.

Assessment

You could ask students to explain their reasoning and to apply the ideas to similar situations. Remember that this activity is more about conceptual understanding than calculation.

Answers to Activity Sheet Questions

Problem 1:

$\$55,000,000 \div \$11,000 = 5,000$ minimum-wage earners

Problem 2:

Teacher's Salary: $\$11,000,000 \times \frac{1}{100} = \$110,000$

6 CEOs $\times \$11,000,000 = \$66,000,000$

$\$66,000,000 \div \$110,000 = 600$ teachers

Alternate method: A teacher makes about $\frac{1}{100}$ what a CEO makes. There would have to be 100 teachers to equal 1 CEO. So for 6 CEOs, $6 \times 100 = 600$ teachers to equal the same salary.

Problem 3:

$40 \div \frac{4}{5} = (40 \div 4) \div \frac{1}{5} = 10 \div \frac{1}{5} = 50$ basketball courts

EXTENSION ACTIVITIES

You might ask students to come up with a well-reasoned argument to justify a common standard method of dividing by a fraction, one of which is often referred to as "invert and multiply."

Fractional Salaries Activity Sheet

Problem One

According to the U.S. Corporate Library, the average salary of a top American CEO in 2005 was $11.75 million. A minimum-wage earner made about $11,000 per year. Imagine there are five CEOs in a small meeting room called the Gold Room. To keep it simple, imagine each one makes $11 million a year, so together they make $55 million annually. Next door in a large meeting room called the Common Room there is a group of minimum-wage earners. How many minimum-wage earners would have to be in the Common Room to equal the same total annual salary as represented in the Gold Room?

Problem Two

A teacher's salary after 10 years' experience is about $\frac{1}{100}$ that of a CEO. Assume there are now six CEOs in the Gold Room, as another CEO has joined the original five. How many teachers would be needed to add up to the total salary currently represented in the Gold Room? See if you can use the fraction $\frac{1}{100}$ in helping you solve the problem.

Problem Three

The cost of a basketball court is about $\frac{4}{5}$ of the cost of the average police officer's salary. The local government is having a problem with young offenders and is trying to decide on a strategy. One suggestion is to hire 40 more police officers. Another is to provide youth with more things to do after school in terms of recreation. For example, a parents group suggests building some basketball courts in the area. How many basketball courts would fit in the budget that would be used to hire 40 police officers for one year? Which do you think would be more useful in reducing crime? (Hint: One possible method is to think about how many $\frac{4}{5}$ "fit" into a single salary.) When you have solved the problem, see if you can solve it another way.

Problem Four

Do some research on the Internet to find statistics and write up a problem of your own similar to the ones above. Then have another team solve it.

Big Ideas for Growing Mathematicians, 2007 © Zephyr Press

A Temperature Experiment

The BIG Idea

Do temperatures tend to change at a steady rate?

Content Areas in This Activity

✔ Measurement
✔ Creating and interpreting graphs
✔ Nonlinear relationships

Process Skills Used in This Activity

✔ Reasoning
✔ Representation

Prerequisite Knowledge and Skills

✔ Reading a thermometer
✔ Two-dimensional graphing

Age Appropriateness

This activity is appropriate for all ages, as long as students can graph ordered pairs.

The Mathematical Idea

It is relatively simple to come up with examples of concrete or real things that students can measure to show linear relationships. Linear relationships are those that change at a constant rate so their graph is a straight line. For example, purchasing a quantity of items for which the price is a certain amount for each item (such as "Show a graph of the total cost of buying 1, 2, 3 . . . 10 chocolate bars if they cost $1.00 each") will yield a linear graph. However, measuring nonlinear relations can be more difficult, such as measuring the height of a falling object over time. The following activity yields a nonlinear relationship that is easy to measure and understand.

Imagine two bowls of water, one cold and another, smaller in size, hot. If you put the container of hot water into the container of cold water, you will see that they both change temperature. Their temperatures will change faster when their temperatures are farther apart, and slower as the two temperatures come closer to being the same. This result will happen no matter the size of bowls or exact initial temperatures, as long as one container has relatively hot water and one contains cold water. Of course, over a longer time the surrounding air will also have an effect. As the graphs converge, we see the resultant temperature from the two containers. These graphs of the change have the shape of what are called exponential functions.

HELPFUL TERMS

Linear relationship: a relationship that changes by the same amount each time. For example, if speed is constant, the distance traveled per hour is the same each hour. The total distance traveled increases by a set (constant) amount added each hour. The graph of distance versus time will be a straight line.

Exponential function: a relationship that changes by multiplying, rather than adding, the previous result by the same number for each interval. For example, if an amount doubles every hour, after three hours you would have $2 \times 2 \times 2$ times as much. The Rice Problem (page 37) is an example of an increasing exponential function. You can also multiply by a number smaller than 1 to make the quantity decrease, which is what is happening with the water temperature.

Making It Work

Objectives

Create and examine the graph of a nonlinear relationship from experimental data.

Materials

✔ 2 bowls, one that will fit inside the other (a bucket and glass will work too)
✔ 2 thermometers
✔ graph paper
✔ water, both hot and cold
✔ clock, watch, or timer with second hand to time one-minute intervals
✔ red and blue pens

Preparation

Hot as well as cold water should be prepared.

Procedure

1. Fill the smaller container with hot water. Take the temperature and record it on a chart.

2. Fill the larger container most of the way with cold water, then place the small container in the larger container. Record the temperature of the larger container.

3. Leave both thermometers in their respective containers and time one minute.

4. Take the temperatures of both bowls of water after a minute. Record both readings on a chart.

5. Keep taking the temperatures at one-minute intervals until the temperatures seem to have stopped changing and are nearly the same. (The length of time this takes will depend on the size of your containers.)

6. Create a line graph using the data. Label time on the horizontal (x) axis and temperature on the vertical (y) axis. Use a blue pen to draw the line for the cold bowl and a red pen to draw the hot-bowl temperatures.

7. Compare your graph with other teams' graphs. How does the resultant temperature change? Do all graphs have the same shape? Why?

Suggestions

Comparing graphs and discussing the common shapes is an important aspect. The point is that the graphs change faster when the temperatures are farther apart. These graphs show relationships that change at different rates depending on the conditions around them.

Assessment

Students should be able to describe what they did and talk about why the water changes temperature more at the start and less later.

EXTENSION ACTIVITIES

Exponential functions govern a lot of natural events, from growth of bacteria (or any population), to decay of radioactivity. Students can do some Web research to look for more sophisticated examples of these functions in our world.

A Temperature Experiment Activity Sheet

If you were driving in a car at 30 miles per hour, and an hour went by, you would have traveled 30 miles. In another hour, you would have traveled another 30 miles. If you graph time and distance, the graph might look like this:

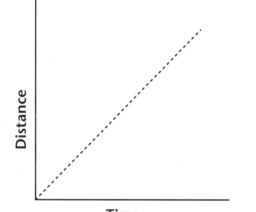

Time

The distance increases by the same amount each hour, and the graph is a straight line. That's why this is called a *linear* relationship.

In this activity you will look at situations that change at rates that are not constant, that is, things change by different amounts each time you measure. (Do you think these graphs will be a straight line?)

Materials

- ✔ 2 bowls, one that will fit inside the other (a bucket and glass will work too)
- ✔ 2 thermometers
- ✔ graph paper
- ✔ red and blue pens
- ✔ water, both hot and cold
- ✔ clock, watch, or timer with a second hand to time one-minute intervals

1 You will need 2 containers, one larger than the other. Fill the smaller container with hot water and record the temperature.

2 Put the other thermometer in the larger container and fill it with cold water. Record this temperature too.

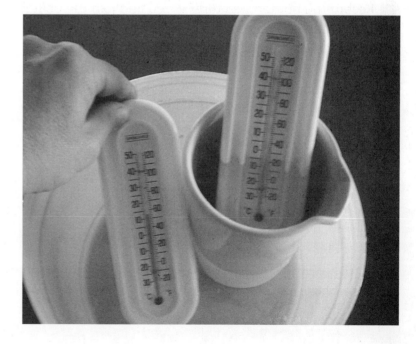

Big Ideas for Growing Mathematicians, 2007 © Zephyr Press

A Temperature Experiment Continued

3 Now place the smaller container inside the bigger one and set the timer for 1 minute (or watch the second hand on a clock).

4 Take the temperatures on the 2 thermometers every minute. Record the temperatures in a chart. Continue recording until the temperatures seem to have stopped changing. This will depend on how big your bowls are and the initial temperatures of the bowls of water.

5 Now graph the results. Use time as the horizontal axis and temperature as the vertical axis.

6 Record the hot temperatures in red and join the points with a red curved line. Do the same for the larger (colder) bowl and join using a blue line.

7 Discuss the following questions:

What happened to the hot water?

What happened to the cold water?

When did the temperatures change the fastest? Why?

Do others' graphs look the same as yours? How are they the same or different?

Would it have made a difference in how the temperatures changed if one of the containers was a lot smaller than the other? How?

What factors could influence the exact location and shape of the curves on the graphs?

Big Ideas for Growing Mathematicians, 2007 © Zephyr Press

Circular Reasoning

The BIG Idea

Circle area and circumference formulas can be found by investigation.

Content Areas in This Activity

✔ Numeracy
✔ Estimation
✔ Measurement—circle area and circumference

Process Skills Used in This Activity

✔ Problem solving
✔ Reasoning

Prerequisite Knowledge and Skills

✔ Multiplication and division
✔ Basic knowledge of decimals
✔ Use and application of simple formulas
✔ Area of a rectangle

Age Appropriateness

This activity is appropriate for all ages as long as children can multiply and use a calculator.

The Mathematical Idea

Teachers sometimes give children the formulas for the circumference and area of circles without explanation as to the formulas' origins or why they make sense. In this activity, children will have a chance to construct these formulas themselves, based on measurement and reasoning.

An important number emerges when you start to work with circles: a number called *pi*. Many people think that pi is exactly 3.14. This value is actually an approximation for pi, whose decimal digits go on infinitely. The term *irrational* is used for such numbers—not because they are crazy (although they almost seem to be!), but because they cannot be written as fractions, or rational numbers. Pi's digits go on forever. That's right, you can never actually write down numbers such as pi exactly! You can approximate pi by writing it as 3.1 or 3.14 or

3.14159. Today, computers can calculate as many digits of an irrational number as you would want, but never all of them.

Pi is one of those special mathematical numbers that gets a name all of its own: the Greek letter π. Pi is important because it is the ratio between the circumference and the diameter of any circle. Children can generally figure out a fairly close estimate of it by measuring the circumference and the diameter of a large circle—the large circles painted on gym floors are wonderful for this—and dividing the circumference by the diameter with a calculator. Averaging several measurements also works well.

Even less understood is where the formula for the area of a circle comes from. Two estimation activities follow. The first uses a method of creating rough circles out of square tiles and looking for a possible formula for the number of tiles.

The second method uses a circle cut up into wedges using a circular set of fraction pieces from a fairly small fraction, such as $\frac{1}{12}$, and the wedges are rearranged to

roughly resemble a rectangle. The dimensions of the rectangle generate the area formula: the rectangle height is the radius (r), and the width is half the circumference, or $\frac{1}{2} \times (2 \pi r)$, which is $\pi \times r$. Multiplying the rectangle's height by the width to determine area is then $r \times (\pi \times r)$, which is πr^2—the formula for a circle's area!

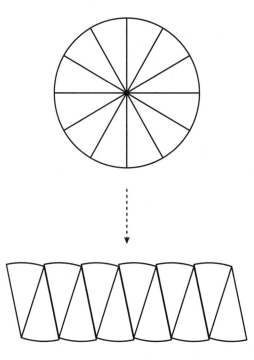

Looking at the figure above, as you imagine using smaller and smaller wedges the picture will get closer and closer to a perfect rectangle. Meanwhile, the width will get closer and closer to half the circumference as you use smaller and smaller wedges. The height is the radius.

HELPFUL TERMS

Circumference: the distance around the circle; its perimeter

Diameter: the distance across the circle through the center

Radius: distance from anywhere on the circumference to the center. This distance will be half the diameter.

Making It Work

Objectives

To establish that the ratio between the circumference and the diameter of any circle appears to be a constant value; to determine an estimated value for this ratio of the circumference to the diameter by exploration; to generate an approximation of the formula for the circumference of the circle given the diameter or the radius; to estimate the area of a circle using tiles; to conjecture a rule that might generate the area; to generate a formula for the circle area based on a construction.

Materials

✔ string
✔ yardstick or meterstick
✔ tiles (48 per student group)
✔ heavy paper and scissors, or a package of circular fraction pieces (one whole cut in 12th or 16ths)
✔ calculator

Preparation

If large circles are not readily available to measure, some circular objects such as round trash cans or circles drawn on the board or the playground with chalk would be useful.

■ If paper circles are to be used for the area, it might help to have these precut into wedges, especially for smaller children.

Procedure

Note: *The activity sheet provided with this lesson could be used as a guide for recording measurements, but sharing of ideas and reasoning is needed as well.*

Circumference Activity

1. Using string and measuring sticks, have children work in groups to measure the circumference and the diameter of a large circle, with each group measuring a different size circle.

2. The students' measurements can be listed on a chart with headings, such as:

Diameter	Circumference

3. It would be best not to write a third column heading on the chart, but rather challenge children to see if they can find a relationship between diameter and circumference from the values listed in their first two columns. Highlighting easy-to-compute values, such as a diameter of about 30 units and a circumference of about 90 units from the list may encourage children to make an initial guess of a ratio of 3. Adding in a third column at this point and asking everyone to determine the ratio of their measurements will solidify the conjecture. Children may need to be reminded that if D × ? = C, then C ÷ D = ? and the ? is the ratio.

4. This activity could be followed by some Internet research on the number pi.

5. The formula C = π × D can also be written C = π × (2 × r) or C = 2 × π × r, which is the more usual form and will be used in the next activity. Before proceeding, familiarize children with the various ways to write the relationship and help them to understand that each one represents the same thing as the others. The symbol π represents a number that is near 3.

Area Estimation Activity

1. Children who have been working recently with pattern rules may be able to come up with a rough formula for the area of a circle by working with tiles. Some quantities of tiles show this more easily than others, due to their divisibility by 4, making a more balanced circle from the four-sided tiles. For example, try making a circle with 12 tiles. The best estimate seems to have a radius of 2:

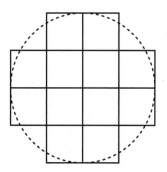

2. Using a similar process, making a circle with 48 tiles, seems to yield a radius of 4. Children may be able to suggest the pattern rule from the data:

radius	number of tiles (area)
2	3 × (2 × 2) = 12
4	3 × (4 × 4) = 48

3. If they attempt to build a circle with radius of 3 using the tiles (omitted in the chart above), they may find that using 28 tiles works better than using the predicted 3 × (3 × 3) or 27 tiles. This might indicate that in fact the conjectured 3 in the formula is really a bit larger than exactly 3. Aha! One can then ask if anyone knows a special number a bit larger than 3.

4. At this point, children might have a working hypothesis that A = 3 × r × r. We will now go on to justify this formula for the circle area further.

Area of a Circle from a Rectangle

1. At this point children can be challenged to create the formula for the area of a circle more deductively, using reasoning based on earlier results. The earlier result they will use is the relationship C = 2 × π × r.

2. Give each group a package of circular fraction pieces or use the template on the activity sheet and have them cut out the wedges. Using the paper template has the advantage that students can write in the radius and the circumference on the sheet before cutting it up, but the cutting process takes time. Alternatively, the paper wedges can be precut.

3. Encourage children to make an approximate rectangle by rearranging the wedges.

4. Discuss what would happen to the exactness of the rectangle if they used smaller and smaller wedges.

5. To determine the rule for the area of a circle, remember what the lengths were on the original circle. It must be established that the height of the newly created rectangle is simply the radius, r, and the width is half the circle circumference—half is on top, and the other half is on the bottom.

6. Children can reason out that the rectangle area must then be

Area (rectangle) = length × width

= length × (½ of circle circumference)
= r × (½ × (2 × π × r))
= r × ½ × 2 × π × r

and since ½ of 2 is just 1,
= r × (π × r),

which they can rearrange to get
= π × r × r

7. Looking back to the conjectured pattern rule, this is close to 3 × r × r, especially when conjectured that the actual number in the formula was really a bit bigger than 3.

Suggestions

This activity is an example of conjecturing and proving in mathematics. It works best if children are encouraged to hypothesize and reason independently as much as possible along the way.

Assessment

Children can be encouraged to explain, orally or in a journal, the reasoning they used in these activities. The results of this activity make a nice presentation to a visitor, such as a parent or school administrator, because although most adults are familiar with these formulas, they would in many cases have no idea how to justify them. It's a piece of cake . . . or pie!

EXTENSION ACTIVITIES

Children may want to do some further investigation on the Web about the origin of these formulas and the historic construction of the number π.

Circular Reasoning Activity Sheet

In this activity you will be investigating some important relationships about circles. You will need to compare ideas with your peers and receive guidance from your teacher as you progress.

Circumference Activity

1 In this activity you will use string and a measuring stick to measure the diameter and circumference of large circles as accurately as possible.

2 Everyone in your group can share their measurements on a chart with headings like these:

Diameter   Circumference

3 Your first task is to search for an estimated pattern rule for the relationship of the diameter to the circumference. If you have measured carefully, the ratio of each diameter measure to its circumference should be about the same. In other words, you are looking for a ratio between the two. There is a special name for this ratio. Record your best estimate of what number times the ratio gives the circumference.

Area Estimation Task

Next, come up with a pattern rule for the area of a circle using square tiles.

1 Using 12 tiles, arrange them in as circular a pattern as you can. How big is the radius of your estimated circle?

2 Now use 48 tiles to make a circle. You should find that the best estimate for a circle from 48 tiles is a radius of 4.

3 Challenge yourself to find a pattern rule for getting from the radius to the area of a circle using your estimates as on this chart. (Hint: You are looking for an area formula. Areas involve multiplying. What happens if you multiply the radius by itself as part of the rule?)

Radius	Estimated Area in Tiles	Pattern Rule Ideas
2	12	
4	48	

4 To help find the rule, you can also try making a circle of tiles with a radius of 3 tiles. Remember, all these areas are estimates so they might be a little off in terms of the rule you are looking for.

5 Share your ideas. If you and your classmates have ideas for a rule, write them down.

Area of a Circle from a Rectangle

1 In this activity your teacher may provide you with a circle cut into wedges, or you may create one by cutting a complete circle into wedges.

Big Ideas for Growing Mathematicians, 2007 © Zephyr Press

Circular Reasoning Continued

2 Before you begin, examine the circle and measure its radius and circumference. Remember that the circumference rule you found earlier is $C = 2 \times \pi \times r$.

3 Arrange the circle wedges into a roughly rectangular shape. The radius of the circle will now be the length of the rectangle.

4 What is the width of the rectangle? (Hint: Find this distance from part of the circle circumference.)

5 The area of a rectangle is length × width. If you were to make the wedges from the circle infinitely small, you can imagine having an exact rectangle. Use your expressions for length and width to find a formula for the circle area.

6 How does your new formula compare with your previously predicted pattern rule?

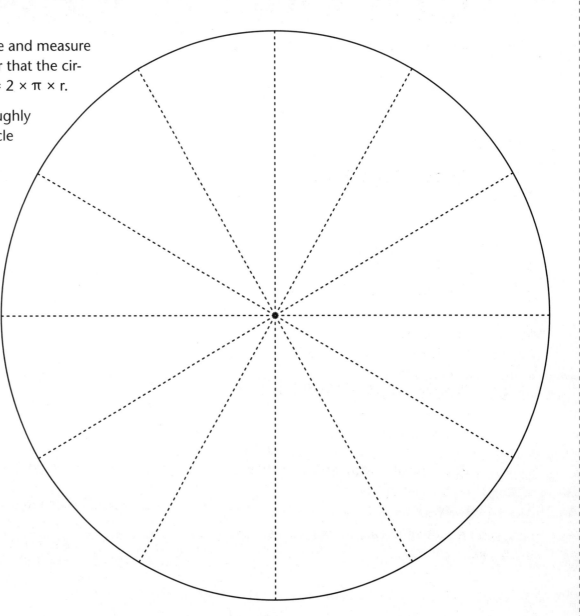

Coins for Compassion

13

The BIG Idea

Big numbers are easier to think about if you compare them to something.

Content Areas in This Activity
✔ Numeracy
✔ Estimation
✔ Measurement of circles

Process Skills Used in This Activity
✔ Problem solving
✔ Reasoning

Prerequisite Knowledge and Skills
✔ Multiplication
✔ Working with large numbers
✔ Circumference measurement

Age Appropriateness

This activity is appropriate for all ages, but children will need the ability to work with large numbers, such as billions.

The Mathematical Idea

Numbers used in calculations about world affairs are often very large and hard to understand. Mathematics has the power to bring such figures to life. Sometimes a concrete metaphor can help.

In this activity, students imagine creating rings of coins around the Earth to create a road containing enough money to end world hunger. One way to tackle the problem is to find the dollar value of one complete ring of coins, and then decide how many rings are needed to reach the target amount of money. Coins can be measured across the diameter. Data for both Imperial and metric solutions are provided. A number of solution methods are of course possible, and students should be encouraged to compare methods. Here are outlines of two possible solutions, one using Imperial units and dimes, and the other using metric units and pennies.

Using Imperial Units and Dimes

■ Dime diameter: approximately ¾ or 0.75 inch

■ Value of 1-foot-long row of dimes: 12 inches ÷ 0.75 × $0.10 = $1.60

■ Value of 1 mile of dimes: 5,280 feet × $1.60 = approximately $8,500

Calculate the circumference of the Earth:

$C = \pi \times D$
$= 3.14 \times 7,900$ miles
$= 24,806$ miles, or about 25,000 miles

Therefore, the dollar value of one ring in dimes is 25,000 × $8,500, or $212,500,000.

Now calculate the number of rings needed to reach the target of $19 billion, an annual estimate to end world hunger.

Rings = $19,000,000,000 ÷ $212,500,000
= 90 rings

So about 90 rings of dimes would do it. This road would be 70 inches, or a little less than 2 yards wide (0.75 inches per dime × 90 dimes is about 70 inches).

Note: *Problems solved with rounded numbers like this are often called Fermi problems, named after Enrico Fermi, the mathematician who made famous this type of application using rounded-off numbers.*

Using Metric Units and Pennies

■ Penny diameter: approximately 2 cm

■ With 100 cm per meter, 1 meter is valued at $0.50 (50 pennies).

■ With 1,000 meters in a kilometer, 1 kilometer of pennies is $500.

Calculate the circumference of the Earth:

$C = \pi \times D$
$= 3.14 \times 12,800$ km
$= 40,192$ km, or about 40,000 km

Therefore, the dollar value of one ring in pennies is 40,000 km × $500/km, or $20,000,000.

Now calculate the number of rings needed to reach the target of $19 billion.

Rings = $19,000,000,000 ÷ $20,000,000
= 950 rings

So nearly 1,000 rings of pennies would be needed for the target amount of money. Since 50 pennies in a line measure about 1 meter, the road would be about 1,000 ÷ 50, or about 20 meters wide.

HELPFUL TERMS

Diameter: distance across a circle through the center

Circumference: distance around a circle; the perimeter

Making It Work

Objectives

Students investigate the number of dimes or pennies needed to create an imaginary ring of coins around the equator. By so doing they work with large numbers to solve a concrete problem, think about various solution methods, work with changing to appropriate units, and use measurement ideas.

Materials

- ✔ coins to measure: pennies and dimes
- ✔ rulers
- ✔ calculators
- ✔ globe to help children visualize rings of coins around the equator

Preparation

None

Procedure

1. Give students the story problem on the activity sheet.

2. Students may either use the Imperial or metric data. Encourage them to work independently or in small groups to solve the problem.

Suggestions

Students may initially encounter difficulties with changing units. Encourage them to work with smaller numbers first to find a method and then apply the method to larger numbers.

Remind students that they are looking for round numbers and they should feel free to round off. They do not need to know an exact number of coins, but rather a rough estimate for the number of rings.

Assessment

Completing the task is sufficient and correctness of solutions could be assessed. Also, if students have done the task using one system of measurement and one type of coin, an assessment task could involve using a different coin.

EXTENSION ACTIVITIES

Students could investigate the number of rings for a different purpose, using the Internet to research data. For example, one estimate is that the United States spends $140 billion a year on advertising. How many rings might this be on the road of coins?

Coins for Compassion Activity Sheet

Imagine that you and your friends have decided to create a challenge from your school to the governments of the world to stop world hunger. Perhaps you have read an estimate on the Internet that an additional $19 billion each year would be enough to eliminate worldwide hunger.

You decide to challenge the world leaders to create an imaginary road paved with coins around the equator. One complete ring around the Earth would make a road that is one coin wide; every time you added another ring it would widen the road by one coin. Approximately how many rings of a certain type of coin would be needed each year to eliminate world hunger? How wide would this road be?

Begin your work by choosing one particular coin, such as a dime or penny. You will need to measure the diameter—the distance across—whatever coin you use. Here is some data to get you started:

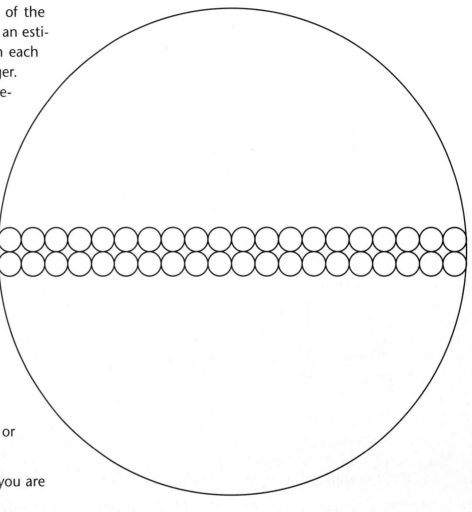

■ Money needed to eliminate world hunger for one year: $19,000,000,000

■ Approximate diameter of the Earth: 7,900 miles or 12,800 km

Round off your numbers as you work. Remember, you are looking for an estimate.

Big Ideas for Growing Mathematicians, 2007 © Zephyr Press

Toothpick Rectangles

14

The BIG Idea

Some rectangles are bigger than others, even if the perimeter is the same.

Content Areas in This Activity

✔ Measurement: area and perimeter of rectangles
✔ Patterning
✔ Graphing

Process Skills Used in This Activity

✔ Reasoning

Prerequisite Knowledge and Skills

✔ Multiplication
✔ Area of a rectangle
✔ Graphing

Age Appropriateness

This activity is appropriate for all children with the above skills.

The Mathematical Idea

A big idea that runs through the middle-school curriculum is the relationship between perimeter and area of two-dimensional shapes, particularly rectangles. In fact, it turns out that in the case of quadrilaterals, the relationship gives rise to a familiar type of relationship that forms a parabolic graph, known as quadratic. (Note the use of the syllable *quad* in each word *quad*rilateral and *quad*ratic.)

The largest possible rectangle in terms of area, for a set perimeter, is in fact a square rectangle. A square is a special type of rectangle; it not only has *opposite* sides equal but *all* sides are equal. (All squares are rectangles, but not all rectangles are squares.) On the other hand, long, skinny rectangles contain relatively less area for the same perimeter.

This geometric idea accounts for why houses that have a relatively square footprint, rather than a long and thin one, are cheaper to build. The idea can also be generalized to three dimensions; containers that are closest to a cube in shape use less packaging for the same volume than longer, thinner packages. (They may also *look* like they hold less, which might not be desired.)

In this activity children build all possible rectangles for a given perimeter and examine the relationship between perimeter and area.

Making It Work

Objectives

Children examine the areas and perimeters of rectangles constructed with toothpicks. They also investigate the relationship between area and perimeter.

Materials

✔ 24 toothpicks per group
✔ grid paper for graphs

Preparation

Count out 24 toothpicks for each group in advance.

Procedure

1. Ask children to build all possible rectangles with the given number of toothpicks (24) and list the length and width on a chart. For this activity, a 1 × 11 rectangle will be considered different than an 11 × 1 rectangle, so groups should list both on their charts.

2. Examine the relationship between length and width for each rectangle. If students know the width, the length is easy to determine, since the perimeter is set at 24 toothpicks/units. The length and width added together make up half the rectangle's perimeter, or 12 toothpicks/units. So if some of the 12 are the length, the rest of the 12 are the width.

3. Record all the combinations on a chart.

4. Once all combinations are made and recorded, students should calculate the area of each rectangle. These are:

Dimensions	Area (l × w)
1 × 11	11 units
2 × 10	20 units

HELPFUL TERMS

Rectangle: a shape with opposite sides equal and four 90-degree interior angles

Square: a rectangle with all four sides equal

Perimeter: the distance around the outside of a two-dimensional shape

Area: the space contained by the perimeter

3 × 9	27 units
4 × 8	32 units
5 × 7	35 units
6 × 6	36 units
7 × 5	35 units
8 × 4	32 units
9 × 3	27 units
10 × 2	20 units
11 × 1	11 units

5. Children should graph the width (on the horizontal x axis) versus the area (on the vertical y axis) and discuss what the graph shows.

Suggestions

To avoid confusion in later discussions, it helps to first agree on which direction is length and which is width.

Encourage children to start organizing their rectangle dimensions in a chart so they can see if they have them all.

Assessment

Children can be asked to do a similar investigation with more toothpicks, for example 32. Be sure to use a number divisible by four to get an exact square with a whole number of toothpicks as the largest rectangle.

EXTENSION ACTIVITIES

If they know the perimeter, children might come up with a pattern rule for the area using just one variable. If the perimeter is 24, and the width is w, then in each half of the rectangle's perimeter, w + length = 12. So, length is the rest of the 12, after students have used up w toothpicks. Thus, the length can be written as 12 − w. And since area is l × w, a formula or pattern rule for the area is w × (12 − w). This, as it turns out, is the equation of the graph of the area. Cool!

Toothpick Rectangles Activity Sheet

Working with a partner, you will be investigating the relationship of area to perimeter for rectangles.

1 Do you think that all the rectangles you can build using exactly 24 toothpicks for the outside edges will have the same area? Or will some be bigger than others? Discuss this in your group before beginning. Make a prediction and write it down. This is called a *conjecture.*

2 Now, use exactly 24 toothpicks to make the outside edge, or *perimeter* of each possible rectangle. Build as many different rectangles as you can. Note: You can consider the two rectangles below to be different, since the length and width are reversed, even if the overall dimensions are the same.

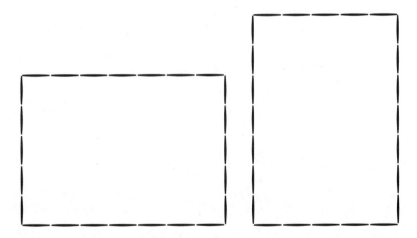

3 Organize your rectangles in a chart. How can you be sure you have them all?

4 If you know the perimeter of a rectangle and the width, is there any choice in the length measurement? Can you explain this?

5 Calculate the area of each rectangle and record each area on the chart. Which one is the biggest? Discuss this in your group.

6 Make a graph of the area versus width for each rectangle you made. Put all the numbers in your chart on the graph as points. Set your graph up like this:

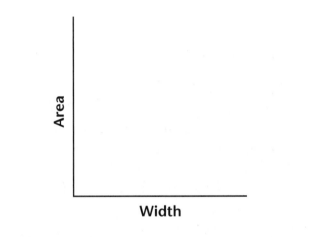

7 Does the graph tell you which rectangle is the largest? How?

8 What do you think the shape would look like if you had more toothpicks? If you have time, try the activity with 32 toothpicks. Can you predict the dimensions and area of the largest rectangle before you begin?

Big Ideas for Growing Mathematicians, 2007 © Zephyr Press

The Stairs Problem

15

The BIG Idea

Algebra—it's all about geometry!

Content Areas in This Activity
✔ Patterning

Process Skills Used in This Activity
✔ Problem solving
✔ Reasoning

Prerequisite Knowledge and Skills
✔ Multiplication
✔ Area models
✔ Use of a variable in a pattern rule

Age Appropriateness

This activity is appropriate for children who have an understanding of a pattern rule with a variable as predicting any term in the pattern.

The Mathematical Idea

A very important formula in mathematics is the formula for adding up a list of numbers in a sequence. The most basic list is the sum of consecutive numbers, such as $1 + 2 + 3 + \ldots + n$. A famous story about this problem is told about the young mathematician Carl Friedrich Gauss who was punished by his teacher by being asked (in the days before calculators!) to add up the numbers from one to one hundred. The teacher was astonished when Gauss had the answer before he reached his seat!

The method Gauss probably used was to pair up the numbers numerically. For example, he noticed that

$$1 + 100 = 101$$
$$2 + 99 = 101$$
$$3 + 98 = 101$$
$$\ldots \text{and so on.}$$

There will be 50 such pairs, ending with $50 + 51$. So, $50 \times 101 = 5,050 \ldots$ which is the answer.

This problem can also be solved concretely with manipulatives. The sum of a list of consecutive numbers can be arranged to form a "staircase" as shown. This is a model of the sum of the numbers from 1 to 4; it can also be seen as the number of blocks needed to build the four-step staircase.

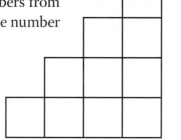

So the question arises, how many blocks are needed to build an n-step staircase?

This problem can be solved in many ways, and it is the richness of the variety of solutions that make this an interesting problem for children. What follow are three different solution methods for the number of blocks in an n-step staircase. Many more are possible!

Solution 1

Make a second staircase of the same size as the original one and fit the two together to form a rectangle.

The size of the rectangle formed by the two staircases will be n × (n + 1). For a four-step staircase, the area of the rectangle will be 4 × 5. Try it! But the rectangle is really two staircases. So, the number of tiles in one staircase is (4 × 5) ÷ 2, or in general, n × (n + 1) ÷ 2.

Solution 2

Build a square of size n, for example, see n = 4 shown.

The shaded tiles, both black and gray, show the original staircase. A formula for the entire square is n^2. Next, find an expression for the unshaded (white) tiles, and then subtract that number from n^2 to get the number of shaded tiles. The formula becomes:

n^2 − number of white tiles = number of tiles in the staircase

So now the problem becomes how to find the number of white tiles. These white tiles are a half of the square (cut diagonally) after removing the black tiles. The black tiles are the diagonal and so there are n of them. So an expression for the number of white tiles is "the square minus the black tiles divided by two," or

$(n^2 − n) ÷ 2$

So n^2 − white tiles = $n^2 − ((n^2 − n) ÷ 2)$

A little algebraic manipulation will show this is really the same as the first formula we found in Solution 1 (if anyone wants it proved algebraically). Here it is:

$$\begin{aligned}
\text{Number of tiles} &= n^2 − ((n^2 − n) ÷ 2) \\
&= n^2 − (n^2 ÷ 2 − n ÷ 2) \\
&= n^2 ÷ 2 + n ÷ 2 \\
&= (n^2 + n) ÷ 2 \\
&= n × (n + 1) ÷ 2
\end{aligned}$$

Cool! Finally a reason to learn all those rules of algebra!

Note: *It is not necessary for children to do this algebraic work; using different forms of the pattern rule are fine. But this is how you as a teacher could check a rule for correctness if you are not sure if it is the same as another one.*

Solution 3

This solution becomes a bit more complicated because you have to use different solutions for odd and even cases of n. But they end up with the same result, though the case of an odd number for n is slightly easier.

First, rearrange the staircase into a shape in which it is easier to count the tiles, a rectangle, by moving the gray tiles as shown. Here is a diagram for when n is 5, an odd number:

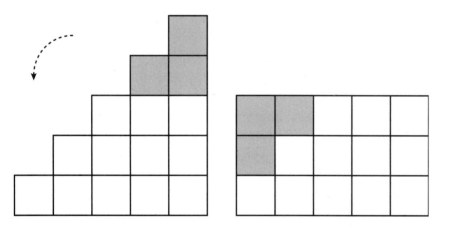

If you calculate the rectangle area, it is the same as the staircase because it's just the staircase tiles rearranged. The rectangle has width of 5 or in general, n. The height is a bit harder. Playing with other *odd*-numbered cases will lead to the expression $(n + 1) \div 2$. Think of it as rounding up to the nearest even number and dividing by 2. Multiplying the width and height gives the same expression we had before, namely, $(n \times (n + 1)) \div 2$.

The rearrangement for the *even*-numbered cases looks different initially, but ends up generating the same formula. Here is the four-step staircase, or n = 4 situation:

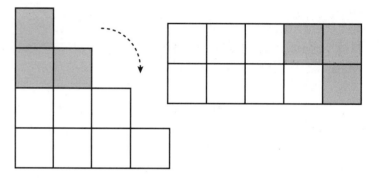

Move the gray tiles a bit differently, rearranging them to add to the width. The width is now $n + 1$, or 5 in this case, and the height is $n \div 2$, or $4 \div 2 (= 2)$ in this case. You might want to try this with the case n = 6 to be sure it always works. So the formula becomes $(n + 1) \times n \div 2$, which is the same as you previously calculated, when rearranged a bit.

HELPFUL TERMS

Recursive solution: the solution for finding the next term. It is not the general solution, but it might be a developmental phase for some children. The recursive solution for the stairs problem might be "add n, plus the number that is 1 less than n, and so on down to 1." For example, for the four-step staircase, the recursive solution is $4 + 3 + 2 + 1$.

Many other solutions are possible, and it is this richness that makes this problem so interesting.

Making It Work

Objectives

Students discover the basic formula for the sum of an arithmetic series using a concrete model and see the equivalence of many solution paths.

Materials

✔ square tiles (or centicubes, or interlocking cubes), up to about 50 per group

Preparation

None

Procedure

1. Children may work individually, in pairs, or in small groups. Encourage them to find more than one solution.

2. The problem can be posed by illustrating a staircase made of blocks. Encourage children to find the total number of tiles or blocks they will need to construct a staircase with any number of steps. To better illustrate the idea, have students build the first few staircases at the same time.

Suggestions

Children who are unable to get started may need to be reminded of some possible strategies. For example, if the number of tiles is hard to count in the current shape, what shape would be easier? How could they rearrange the tiles to count them more easily? Can they find a method of rearranging that works with *any* number of steps? The suggestion of using two staircases can be offered if children are getting frustrated.

Assessment

Children could be encouraged to write out their thinking from their solution to show their understanding, or they could explain it orally.

EXTENSION ACTIVITIES

Once children have solved the problem one way, encourage them to solve it using another method.

Another related problem is to find the sum of a list of odd (or even) numbers. That is, they could build a model for and solve either 1 + 3 + 5 + . . . or 2 + 4 + 6 + . . .

The Staircase Problem Activity Sheet

In this activity you will be working with tiles to solve a patterning problem. You need to find the number of tiles or blocks needed to build a staircase with any number of steps. Here is a staircase with 5 steps, and you can see that 1 + 2 + 3 + 4 + 5 = 15, the number blocks or tiles needed.

1 Find a rule for the number of tiles in the staircase with any number of steps. Use n to represent the number of steps.

2 Here's a hint: try working with a specific number of tiles. Rearranging the tiles or adding more might help.

3 Look for a way to calculate the number of tiles using your new shape, and see if the method would work with a different number of stairs.

Gumball Boxes

16

The BIG Idea

Do more but smaller things always fill a space better?

Content Areas in This Activity

✔ Numeracy
✔ Measurement
✔ Areas of rectangles and circles

Process Skills Used in This Activity

✔ Visualization
✔ Reasoning
✔ Problem solving

Prerequisite Knowledge and Skills

✔ Multiplication
✔ Volume of a rectangular prism
✔ Volume formula for a sphere
✔ Area for a circle

Age Appropriateness

This activity is appropriate for seventh-grade students and above, or students comfortable with the prerequisite knowledge and skills.

The Mathematical Idea

A central notion of calculus is that a curved flat space can be filled more accurately by estimating it with narrower and narrower rectangles. When the rectangles are infinitely narrow, they can be made to fill a given area perfectly.

> ### HELPFUL TERMS
>
> **Sphere:** a perfectly round ball; the volume of the sphere is determined by the formula $\frac{4}{3} \times \pi \times r^3$, where r is the radius of the sphere.

This seems reasonable when looking, for example, at the shapes below. The narrower rectangles are a better approximation of the area. If you imagine using very narrow rectangles, you can almost think of the top edges of the rectangles as starting to resemble a curve.

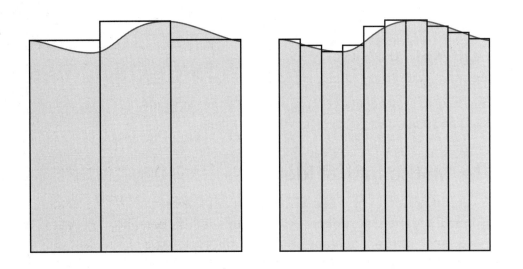

In this activity students will look at something that seems to follow a similar idea, yet contains a surprise. Imagine taking a box, such as a tissue box, and filling it with large solid gumballs. You can calculate the volume of gum in each gumball using the formula for the volume of a sphere. So, for example, if they are 2-inch gumballs, the radius on each is 1 inch. So the volume of each gumball, using the volume of a sphere formula, is $\frac{4}{3} \pi r^3$ or about $\frac{4}{3}$ (3.14) $(1)^3$, which is about 4.2 cubic inches of gum per gumball.

To calculate the amount of gum in the box, multiply the amount of gum per gumball by the number of gumballs that fit in the box. The total volume in the box is calculated as length × width × height, and the amount of empty space is the total volume of the box minus the total amount of gum. This process can be repeated for any size of gumball.

Now imagine that the gumball size is getting smaller and smaller. Eventually each gumball could be like a tiny round bead. As you repeat the calculation with smaller and smaller gumballs, what happens to the amount of gum and the amount of empty space in the box? (You may want to skip ahead and actually try the activity before reading further. Sometimes knowing the answer spoils the fun of the activity!) What do you think will happen to the amount of empty space as the balls get very tiny? Can you visualize this?

As children continue to calculate, they will notice an amazing thing: the amount of gum (and the amount of space) in the box *stays the same,* even with smaller balls of gum! It does seem surprising that tiny but spherical grains of sand would include the same amount of total empty space as a box of larger balls! After the activity, the surprising conclusion is that even though smaller rectangles fill a curved flat space better, smaller round balls do not fill a rectangular volume any better.

The extension activity suggests trying the idea in two dimensions. In fact, smaller circles do not fill a rectangle any better than larger ones. This surprising result has to do with the shapes being used—circles or spheres, which stay circular, even when they get smaller and smaller.

Making It Work

Objectives

Students use formulas for the volume of rectangular prisms and spheres, as well as reasoning and problem solving, to obtain a surprising result.

Materials

The activity will be most satisfying if done with actual materials. The photographs provided show gumballs with diameters of about 2 inches, 1 inch, and ½ inch. In this case, the following materials are needed:

✔ rectangular box, no larger than a tissue box
✔ enough gumballs to fill it with at least three different sizes of balls (varying sizes of Styrofoam balls would work too, but might be less fun!)
✔ ruler

Preparation

None

Procedure

1. Begin with a discussion of the idea of rectangles approximating a flat area. Lead students to the observation that it is reasonable to conclude that smaller rectangles will provide a better approximation for a curved area.

2. Introduce students to the gumball problem and ask them to make a conjecture about the amount of gum and the amount of empty space as the balls get smaller and smaller.

3. Ask students to work on the problem independently or in pairs to verify or dispute the conjecture.

Assessment

If students can show and explain their calculations, they are providing evidence of understanding.

EXTENSION ACTIVITIES

Students may assume that the reason the balls don't approximate the volume better as they get smaller, even though rectangles approximate a curved shape better as they get smaller, is that the problem is three-dimensional. If they mention this, have them translate the problem to two dimensions and investigate. For example, is the amount of area inside the circles and in the rest of the square more, less, or the same in each picture below?

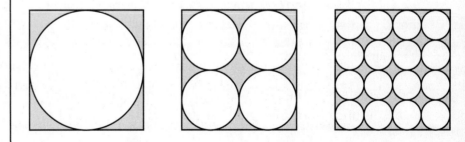

Gumball Boxes Activity Sheet

Smaller and smaller rectangles are a shape that mathematicians sometimes use to measure the area in a flat but curved shape. The smaller the rectangle is, the better the estimate for the area.

In this activity you will look at a problem in three dimensions. You will use a box filled with gumballs of various sizes to see if the smaller ones fill the box more completely (with less empty space) than larger ones.

1 Begin by making a conjecture. This is a prediction of what you believe will happen. Decide if you think that as you fill the box with smaller and smaller gumballs, you will fill it more completely or less completely. That is to say, will you have more gum and less empty space, as the gumballs get smaller? Or will you have less gum? Or will the amount stay the same?

2 Once you've made your conjecture, it's time to measure. Use a small rectangular box, such as a tissue container, for your measurements. Your teacher will provide several sizes of spheres (round objects such as gumballs), enough of each size to fill the box.

3 Fill the box with the largest size of the gumballs. Count them.

4 Calculate the amount of gum in each gumball. Use the formula for the volume of a sphere: ⅓ π r³. (Use 3.14 to approximate π.) The letter *r* stands for the radius, which is the distance from the center to the outside surface. The easiest way to measure the radius is to measure the distance across the ball, the diameter, and then take half of it.

5 Once you have calculated the volume of gum in one ball, multiply it by the number of gumballs in the box to determine the total amount of gum in the box.

6 Next, calculate the volume of the box by measuring it and multiplying the dimensions to find volume.

7 Determine how much empty space is left in the box by subtracting the amount of gum from the overall volume. You may want to record your information on a chart.

8 Repeat steps 3 through 7 with at least two other sizes of gumballs.

9 What can you conclude from your observations and calculations? Does the data support your conjecture? Why do you think this result is the case? Predict what would happen if you kept going with smaller and smaller gumballs.

Big Ideas for Growing Mathematicians, 2007 © Zephyr Press

The Medicine Experiment

17

The BIG Idea

Functions of the body are modeled well by mathematics!

Content Areas in This Activity

✔ Numeracy
✔ Estimation
✔ Patterning

Process Skills Used in This Activity

✔ Reasoning
✔ Problem solving

Prerequisite Knowledge and Skills

✔ Multiplication

Age Appropriateness

This activity is appropriate for all ages.

The Mathematical Idea

A relatively new branch of mathematics called *dynamical systems* turns out to be very useful for modeling body functions and other natural processes. Such systems follow recursive reasoning, which means that the result of one event becomes the starting condition for the next. For example, if you take some medicine and four hours later there is still some of it in your body, the new dose you take at that point will add to the amount of medicine you still have in your system. Taking medicine and eliminating it forms what in mathematics can be called an *iterative process*.

HELPFUL TERMS

Iterative process: a mathematical process in which the result of one event becomes the starting point for the next event

---

The following experiment models a similar iterative process. A mathematical model can be set up to predict what will happen over time when a person takes medicine and his or her body cleanses it out of the blood with the help of the kidneys.

In this model you have a starting amount—the amount of medicine in the initial dose—and then a rule for what is changing. For example, it might be noted that a particular type of medicine is broken down and cleansed out of the blood at a rate of 25 percent of the amount per hour. This could mean that either 25 percent is being *removed* each hour, or 75 percent (the rest) is *remaining* after each hour. Fractions could be used as well, or decimals, in your model. (It's always a good idea to show equivalent ways of calculating things because it encourages deeper levels of student understanding.)

In this experiment, students start out with 16 milliliters of medicine. Using this model, they see that after one hour there is 0.75 × (16 milliliters), or 12 milliliters, left. After the second hour there is 0.75 × (12 milliliters), or 9 milliliters, left. After three hours there is 0.75 × (9 milliliters), or 6.75 milliliters, left. They could continue this progression to see how long it would take to get below a certain level.

A more complicated model might include taking a new dose of medicine after four hours. This would yield numbers such as in the chart below.

Students can extend the chart or change the model as required. They could also use a computer spreadsheet. They could analyze the data to discuss why, for example, certain medicines carry "maximum daily dosage" warnings on their labels.

Hour number	Previous dosage	New dose, if required	Dosage total	Remaining dosage after one hour (0.75 × amount)
1	16		16	12
2	12		12	9
3	9		9	6.75
4	6.75	16	22.75	17.06
5	17.06		17.06	12.80

Making It Work

Objectives

Students concretely model a bodily function and then create a mathematical model.

Materials

✔ 2 pails (or an ice cream bucket and one pail); white pails work best
✔ small bottle of liquid food color
✔ 1-tablespoon (or 16-milliliter) measure
✔ measuring cup

✔ water

✔ calculator or spreadsheet

Preparation

Students can do the setup once supplies are ready.

Procedure

1. Groups of four work well for this activity. If possible, have children do the activity outside to avoid messy spills. Have an extra bucket of clear water on hand if a hose is not available. Several groups can share the clear water.

2. Students follow the activity sheet to model medicine being taken and then cleansed from the body.

3. Children should repeat the process enough times with the physical materials that they are able to understand it fully when they go to model it using mathematics without the materials.

Suggestions

Have students record their observations of the color left in the pail after each iteration. They could also create a chart of calculations as they perform each concrete step.

Assessment

Once students have completed the concrete model, assess their understanding of the mathematical model by asking them to redo the experiment mathematically using different parameters, such as a different initial dose or different rate of purification. Facilitating a discussion of the effects of real drugs on the human body could help them make connections to science or health.

EXTENSION ACTIVITIES

You might ask students more probing questions; for example, if someone took the medicine for a particular number of days and then stopped, how long would it take for the amount in the body to fall below a certain level? Using data they find on the Internet about certain medicines or drugs would make the work more realistic.

The Medicine Experiment Activity Sheet

In this activity you will be working in groups to model what your body does when you take a dose of medicine. Mathematics will help you to analyze the results and make predictions.

1 Model the blood in a person's body by measuring 4 liters (about 16 cups) of water into a bucket or ice cream pail. (If you are interested in finding out the actual amount of blood in the human body, you can do an Internet search.)

2 Now model that person taking a dose of medicine by adding 16 milliliters (or 1 tablespoon) of medicine in the form of liquid food color. Notice the color in the pail after you have added the medicine.

3 In your model, the body cleanses out the medicine in the blood at a rate of 25 percent per hour. This means that after 1 hour, 75 percent of the original dose will be left. Model this by removing one liter—¼ of the total, which would be 4 cups—of colored water, dumping it into a second bucket (or the sink), which represents the bladder, and replacing this colored water with 1 liter (or 4 cups) of clear

water, which the blood absorbs from the stomach. Now the model body still contains 4 liters of water, but less medicine.

4 Repeat this process for a 4-hour interval and make a chart to show how much medicine is left in the body at the end of each hour. What does the color look like after 4 hours?

5 Now that you have the idea, investigate this process using a mathematical model, without actually continuing the experiment using water. Here are some questions to consider:

- Using the model, how much medicine will be left after 12 hours?

- When will there be less than 1 milliliter of medicine left in the body?

- What would happen if we changed the model to take a new dose of medicine every 4 hours? How much would there be now after 12 hours?

- If this medicine is considered safe in the body up to a total amount of 24 milliliters, is this medicine safe to take over a longer period? Why or why not? (A spreadsheet might help with this analysis.)

Big Ideas for Growing Mathematicians, 2007 © Zephyr Press

Fabulous Fractals

18

The BIG Idea

Fractals—the geometry of infinite patterns—are the coolest!

Content Areas in This Activity
✔ Geometry
✔ Patterning

Process Skills Used in This Activity
✔ Creativity
✔ Reasoning

Prerequisite Knowledge and Skills
✔ None

Age Appropriateness

This activity is appropriate for all ages.

The Mathematical Idea

Mathematics has existed for thousands of years with basic geometry such as that of the Ancient Greek mathematician Euclid. Euclidian geometry is based on points, lines, and shapes, as well as deductive reasoning. The shapes are imaginary; perfect straight lines with no width don't really exist. Very recently—in mathematical terms, "very recently" means only a few decades ago—a man named Benoit Mandelbrot invented a new kind of geometry called *fractal geometry*. Some of Mandelbrot's story is told in the activity sheet to follow.

Mandelbrot coined the word *fractal* to describe his new geometric shapes. He observed that some shapes, such as the straight line, look the same when you move closer and closer to them. But other shapes, such as the circle or sphere, appear different as you move closer. For example, the moon might look round to an astronaut in space. As the astronaut comes closer to moon and lands on it, it would appear less and less round. Mandelbrot defined fractals as shapes that look the same as we get closer and closer to them, but are not straight lines.

A quick Web search for the phrase *fractal geometry* will provide many astoundingly beautiful images. It is not necessary to understand the mathematics that underlies them to appreciate them. Students getting a glimpse of these shapes are often fascinated.

Even more exciting are the examples of fractals in nature and other areas of science. Maple leaves, ferns, snowflakes, some root structures, and even the human bloodstream are examples of structures that follow fractal rules. Fractals, which were initially created for amusement, have turned out to model many natural phenomena much better than standard geometries!

Making It Work

Objectives

Students investigate fractals on the Web and in nature and then create one of their own.

HELPFUL TERMS

Fractal: a shape created by applying the same mathematical rule on a smaller and smaller scale

---

Materials

✔ Materials will vary depending on students' choices of model. Paper and colored pencils, crayons, or markers provide a good starting point.

Preparation

It might be interesting to have some examples of fractals in nature available for students to examine. For example, ferns and maple leaves follow fractal rules. Other objects, such as the dream catchers made by Native Americans, are also examples of fractals.

Procedure

1. Students can begin by examining fractals on the Web. Sites that allow students to zoom in and out on images are particularly interesting. Two classic fractals are the Sierpinski triangle and the Koch snowflake, for which the rules are easily discernible.

2. Challenge students to create their own fractals, based on rules of their own choosing.

Suggestions

Enjoyment and creativity are important in this activity. Challenge students to explain clearly the rule on which their fractal is based. For example, the rule "start with a square, make a new square using half the side lengths of the previous one, and rotate it 45 degrees at a vertex" might define a relatively straightforward fractal.

Assessment

Students should be able to explain clearly the fractal rules they used.

EXTENSION ACTIVITIES

The possibilities are unlimited! Make use of the Web for inspiration. There is even fractal music! Try finding and listening to some.

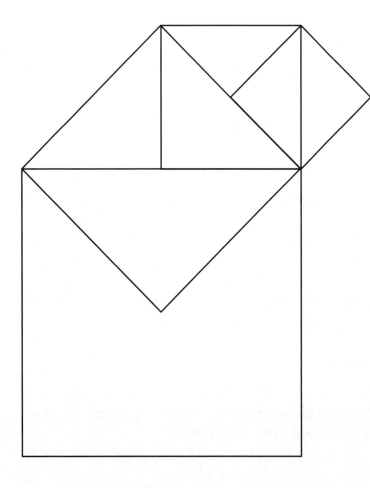

Fabulous Fractals Activity Sheet

For centuries, mathematicians have been doing mathematics by hand. Recently, though, they have begun to use computers to help them in their work, and this is allowing the creation of whole new areas of mathematics. One example is fractal geometry.

To get an idea of what a fractal is, you might want to do a quick Web search for the term *fractal geometry* or *fractal.* You will find dozens of gorgeous images that really need to be seen to be believed! After you do this search, you can read on to find the story of how these images were discovered by a man named Mandelbrot.

The Story of Benoit Mandelbrot and His Discovery of Fractals

Most of the mathematics you learn in elementary school and high school has been known for hundreds of years. Fractal geometry, on the other hand, has only been around a few decades. Already it is showing great potential for practical applications and for modeling things in nature.

Benoit Mandelbrot was a young mathematician working in France with a very famous group of theoretical mathematicians. He did not find this work stimulating, so he moved to the United States and began working for IBM. He enjoyed playing with computer images in his spare time. One day, using a fairly simple mathematical rule applied over and over, he created an amazing image that is now known as the Mandelbrot Set. Perhaps you have already seen this image on the Web; if not, you may want to do a search. As you zoom in on this image, you see the same shapes occurring on smaller and smaller scales. This image is the hallmark of fractal geometry.

Mandelbrot defined the term *fractal* for us. Imagine a straight line. As you look closer and closer at a straight line, it looks the same. Now imagine a circle or a sphere like the Earth. From outer space it looks round. As you move closer and closer, it changes. It begins to look flat. Mandelbrot defined a fractal as a shape that stays the same as you get closer and closer, but is not a straight line.

Many things in nature follow fractal-like rules. Snowflakes, ferns, maple leaves, some root structures, and even the human bloodstream can be effectively modeled by fractal geometry. Can you think of others? Mandelbrot discovered fractals simply by having fun in his spare time!

To create a fractal, you start with a basic shape. Then you apply a rule to change it. Then you apply the rule again to the result of the last change, and so on.

The Activity

In this activity, you will be creating your own fractal. For inspiration, consider the quilt pattern shown or the dream catcher from Native American culture.

Well-known fractals you might find on the Web, including the Sierpinski triangle or the Koch snowflake, might also give you ideas. You might want to use colored paper or col-

Big Ideas for Growing Mathematicians, 2007 © Zephyr Press

Fabulous Fractals Continued

ored markers. To make a fractal, you need a clearly defined rule you can apply over and over. A more complicated rule may result in a more interesting shape. The only limitation is your own creativity! Have fun! Remember, you are on the leading edge of mathematical discovery!

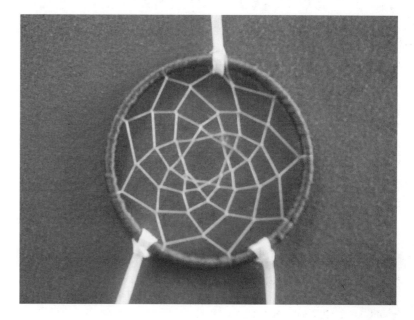

Big Ideas for Growing Mathematicians, 2007 © Zephyr Press

Triangular Tessellations

19

The BIG Idea

Tiling patterns work with triangles and hexagons too!

Content Areas in This Activity
✔ Transformational geometry
✔ Plane geometry
✔ Tiling patterns

Process Skills Used in This Activity
✔ Creative thinking
✔ Reasoning

Prerequisite Knowledge and Skills
✔ Basic idea of rotations and reflections

Age Appropriateness

This activity is appropriate for all ages.

The Mathematical Idea

A tessellation pattern is a shape that will continue to exactly cover a flat surface, no matter the size of the surface. The angles at which the vertices of the tessellating shapes meet must add up to 360 degrees to cover the surface perfectly. A square is a simple tessellation because four 90 degree angles meet at each intersection point and add up to 360 degrees. This explains why squares work well to tile a wall. In *Big Ideas for Small Mathematicians* students looked at tessellations made from squares. In the following activity they will use a hexagon (in which there are six equilateral triangles) as the basic shape. Hexagons also tessellate because three angles of 120 degrees also add up to 360 degrees.

Examples on the Web will show you a number of different methods to create these shapes. Two of the simplest methods are used in the activity. In the first pattern, the same shape is drawn on every single triangle side within the hexagon. This will work as long as the newly drawn line is rotationally symmetric around the midpoint of each side. Here are examples of what that looks like:

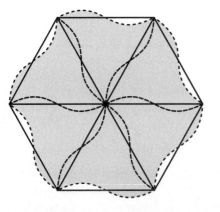

Both new curves are rotationally symmetric around the line's midpoint.

As before, the outside edge of each hexagon has rotational symmetry about the midpoint of each segment. However, the edges inside the hexagon—the inner dotted lines—simply show rotational symmetry about the center of the hexagon. (Reflections could also be used on each side.) This layout allows a little more freedom in the design, as in many of M. C. Escher's drawings, which are available for viewing on the Web.

One method of tessellating the triangles within each hexagon is to create a rotationally symmetric shape on each edge, as in the diagram below.

Center of hexagon

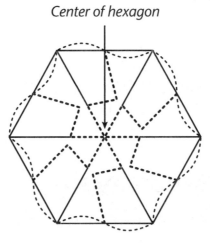

In fact, when many hexagons are put together to create a tessellation, a different shape can be used for the border of the hexagon from the one used for the spokes within each hexagon. The picture to the right illustrates another method of creating a hexagonal tessellation.

Students can investigate Escher's hexagonal tessellations on the Web, superimpose the hexagons and triangles on the printed pages with a pencil, and further investigate these and other methods for creating tessellating designs. You may wish to explain to them some of the methods just outlined or leave them to discover them on their own depending on the time available and skill level of students.

Making It Work

Objectives

Students create their own hexagonal tiling pattern in possible preparation for creating their own kaleidocycle, if desired, in chapter 20.

Materials

- ✔ pencil
- ✔ ruler
- ✔ hexagon pattern sheet (several copies per student)
- ✔ colored pencils, crayons, or markers
- ✔ Internet access (and printer, if possible)

HELPFUL TERMS

Tessellation: a shape that will completely cover a flat surface when used as a tiling pattern, with no overlaps or gaps. The important idea is to have the total angles of the pieces that meet at each point add up to 360 degrees.

Hexagon: a polygon with six equal sides and interior angles. Although technically a hexagon can have any length sides or interior angles, regular hexagons (the ones with all six equal sides and interior angles) are often referred to simply as hexagons.

Vertex: the point where the sides of a shape meet

Preparation

None

Procedure

1. The best way to pique students' interest is by having them search "hexagonal tessellations" on the Web. Many wonderful sites are available; those with M. C. Escher reproductions are especially illuminating.

2. Challenge students to think about the different ways they can create a tessellation with hexagons.

3. If possible, print out tessellating patterns and sketch the triangles in the hexagons. Children should look for the place with a rotated pattern—this will be the center of the hexagon where the triangles meet.

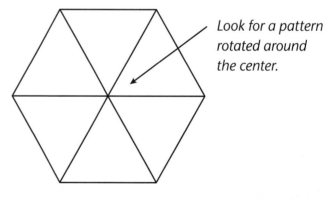

Look for a pattern rotated around the center.

4. Students must then identify what is needed to make the pattern continue. Several possibilities exist; they are suggested previously in the Mathematical Idea section.

Once they choose a design type, they can begin creating it on the template and then color and decorate it.

Suggestions

Students love to create a recognizable design, such as an animal. Suggest they start with a simple design and then gradually refine it to look more and more like an identifiable figure.

Assessment

Students should be able to describe the rule or method they used to create their tessellation pattern. It should be a pattern that, if continued, could cover a much larger surface.

EXTENSION ACTIVITIES

Some pattern types are harder than others. Students can look for other design rules and create new patterns.

Triangular Tessellations Activity Sheet

You may have used squares or rectangles previously to create a tiling pattern, or *tessellation.* Hexagons are also tessellation patterns. Have you seen a bathroom or building with hexagonal tiles?

1 Begin by doing a Web search for hexagonal tessellations, and look especially for M. C. Escher sites. Print out a few. To begin, choose a few that look a bit simpler.

2 Examine the printouts by identifying the hexagons in each and outline them with a pencil. It may help to locate the center of each hexagon—it will be the place around which a shape seems to be rotated six times. Examine each printout to look for the methods used.

3 Now it is time to create your own tessellation. In some hexagonal tessellations, you will see that the same shape has been drawn on each edge, and the shapes have rotational symmetry. One simple rule for creating these hexagonal tessellations is to mark the center of each line. Do this on one line segment of the hexagonal grid sheet.

4 Next, draw a shape on one half of the line segment and then rotate this shape 180 degrees around the midpoint for the other half. Each side now has rotational symmetry within itself. The illustration has this property. The circular markers show the midpoint of each line. One half of each line is a 180 degree rotation of the other part. The lines also rotate around the center of the hexagon itself.

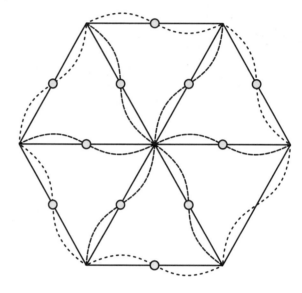

5 Other tessellation methods are possible and you can use your Web printouts to discover these. Decide on a method to follow and create several designs of your own, possibly using additional copies of the hexagonal grid sheet. You can make an even larger design by taping several copies of the grid sheet together.

6 You can also gradually adjust your drawings to look like a particular shape or animal. (Think of the six points of the hexagon as four arms, a head, and a tail.) Choose your favorite and color and decorate it. In chapter 20 you will use your methods to decorate your own kaleidocycle!

Big Ideas for Growing Mathematicians, 2007 © Zephyr Press

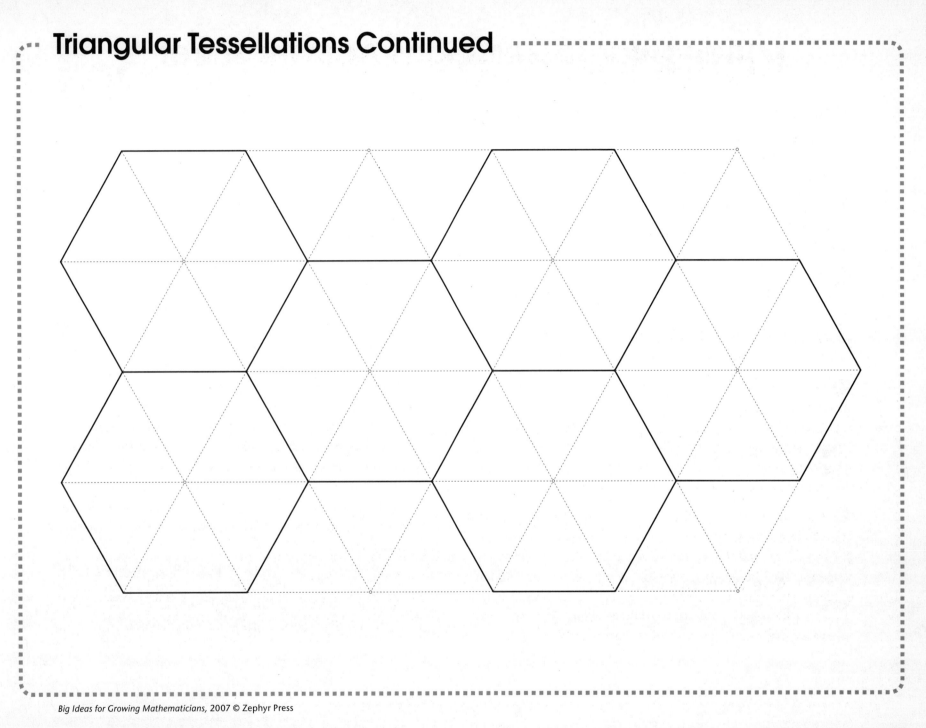

Kaleidocycles

20

The BIG Idea

Geometry is amazing!

Content Areas in This Activity
✔ Spatial reasoning
✔ Polyhedra

Process Skills Used in This Activity
✔ Creativity
✔ Visualization

Prerequisite Knowledge and Skills
✔ Knowledge of triangular tiling patterns (see chapter 19)

Age Appropriateness

This activity is appropriate for all ages.

The Mathematical Idea

Geometry yields some amazing phenomena! In this relatively simple activity, students only need two pages of heavy paper to construct a fascinating three-dimensional object that will continuously rotate inward toward the center or back out toward its outer edges. Though it is a toy, it relies on some interesting geometry to work.

This object has a number of names. Sometimes it is called a *kaleidocycle* due to its rotational properties. It is also referred to as a *hexaflexigon*—it is flexible, and contains hexagon shapes—as well as a *rotatable ring of tetrahedra,* since it rotates and is built from tetrahedra, which is the plural of tetrahedron. This activity reinforces the idea that math can be amazing, surprising, and just plain fun!

Students are given a two-page template, as provided with the activity sheet. The activity works better if the template can be photocopied onto cardstock, rather than standard paper. Students can decorate the triangles according to what they learned in chapter 19, using M. C. Escher–like patterns. The shapes then need to be cut out, folded and scored, and glued according to the directions on the activity sheet. The finished kaleidocycle will rotate continuously and provide lots of interest.

Making It Work

Objectives

The main purpose of this activity is to see geometry at its finest: enjoyable and fascinating!

Materials

✔ photocopy of the two-page template in the activity sheet for each student; use cardstock if possible
✔ scissors
✔ tape
✔ glue stick
✔ colored pencils, crayons, or markers

Preparation

The template should be photocopied on cardstock in advance.

Procedure

1. Cut out the two pages of the template along their outer, solid outlines.

2. Attach the two cutouts securely to one another using a glue stick or tape, face out, along Edge A. Allow the glue to dry completely.

3. Fold each template along its dashed lines. For all the *horizontal* lines, fold the template toward you so that the face of the template is on the *inside*. For all the *diagonal* lines (in both directions), fold the template so that the face of the template is on the *outside*.

4. Use your fingernail or scissors to strongly score each fold to make the creases sharp.

5. At this point, you can decorate the outer face as you wish. It will be easier now than after it is fully constructed.

HELPFUL TERMS

Kaleidocycle: a shape made from triangles formed into a tube and then joined in a ring; also called a *hexaflexigon* or *rotatable ring of tetrahedra*.

Tetrahedron: a three-dimensional shape made from four triangles. The plural is *tetrahedra*.

6. Starting from one end, glue each of the three shaded side tabs to the back of the other side. The end result will be a snakelike cylinder of six triangular segments. Allow the glue to dry.

7. Bend the triangular segments into a ring so that the two end tabs on one end can be inserted into the opening on the other end. Tape the ends together.

8. Once secure, you should be able to gently rotate the kaleidocycle in upon itself.

Suggestions

It is important that students make nice sharp folds, so the ring will rotate freely. All lines must be folded, so that the ring will easily form into the shape.

Assessment

Completion of the kaleidocycle is all that is required.

EXTENSION ACTIVITIES

Students can research and create other types of hexaflexigons by looking on the Web.

Kaleidocycles Activity Sheet

Geometry makes a lot of cool things possible! In this activity, you will be creating a fun toy with a number of names. Sometimes it is called a *kaleidocycle* because it rotates, or cycles. Sometimes it is called a *hexaflexigon* because it contains hexagons, and it is flexible. And sometimes it is called a *rotatable ring of tetrahedra* because it rotates and contains tetrahedron shapes (*tetrahedra* is the plural).

1 Use the two pattern sheets, or templates, your teacher provides.

2 Cut out the templates on the outer, solid cutting lines.

3 Glue (or tape) the two cutouts securely to one another, face out, along Edge A. Allow the glue to dry completely.

4 Fold each template along its dashed lines. For all the *horizontal* lines, fold the template toward you so that the face of the template is on the *inside.* For all the *diagonal* lines (in both directions), fold the template so that the face of the template is on the *outside.*

5 Use your fingernail or a pair of scissors to make sure each fold is a sharp, crisp fold.

6 Color the face of the templates. If you have already made triangular tessellations in chapter 19, you can decorate your kaleidocycle in a cool way.

7 Now you are ready to fold your kaleidocycle. First, bring the two long sides together to make a long snakelike cylinder, as shown to the right. If all the lines are folded,

it will easily bend into this shape.

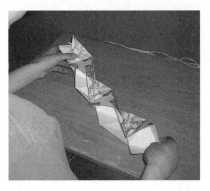

8 Starting at one end, put glue on each shaded side tab and press the opposite side on top, making sure the edges line up. Reinforce with tape and let the glue dry. Repeat for the other two side tabs. It should look like a long, skinny, wiggly shape, with six triangular segments.

9 Now bring the shape around to form a ring. Fit the end tabs into the open slot at the other end of the snake. Push them into the slot and tape the edge securely.

10 You should now have a ring that you can carefully rotate inward or outward as many times as you want. Have fun!

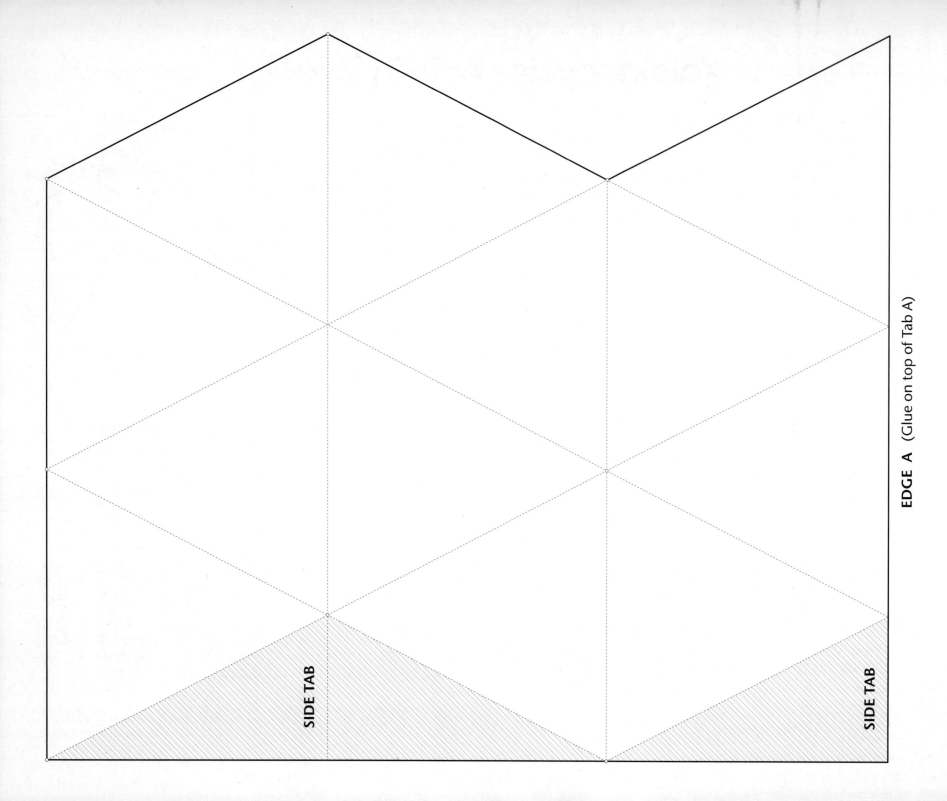

SIDE TAB

SIDE TAB

EDGE A (Glue on top of Tab A)

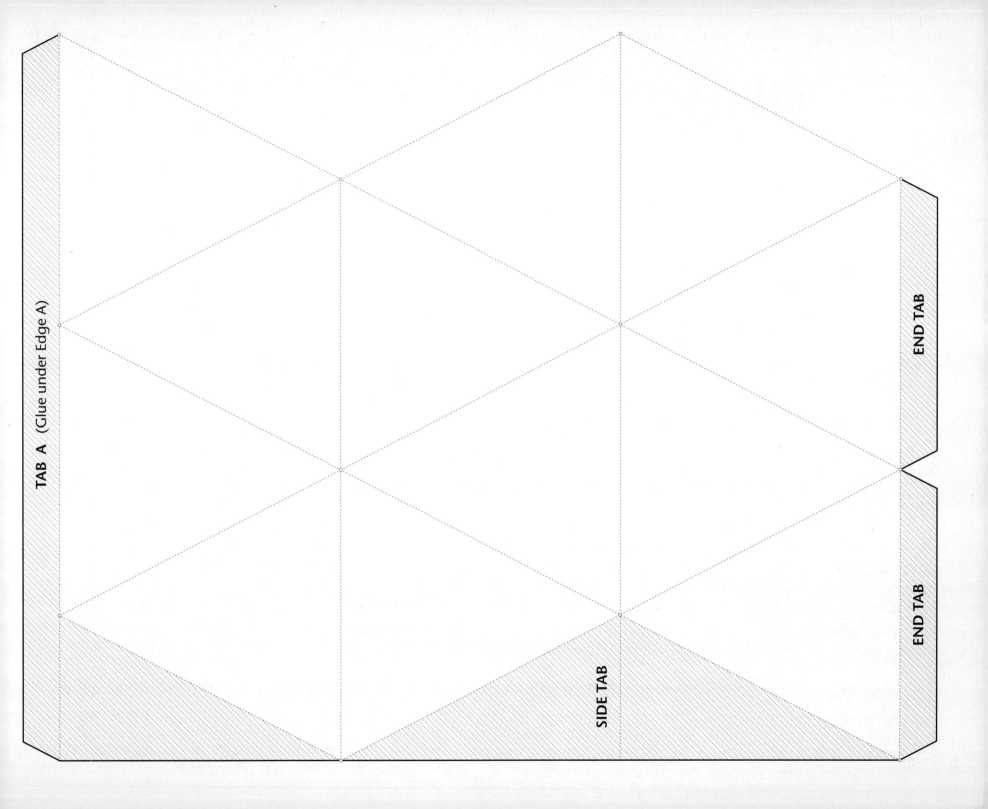

TAB A (Glue under Edge A)

END TAB

END TAB

SIDE TAB

Glossary

area: the space contained by the perimeter of a two-dimensional shape

average or (more formally) mean: the calculation used to find this number is "add all the numbers in a list and divide by how many there are." More conceptually, the mean is the "equal share" of the total amount.

binary numbers: numbers that are powers of 2, e.g., 8 or 64

binomial: an expression with two terms in it, such as "n + 2"

column: one vertical set of cells or dots

circumference: the distance around a circle; its perimeter

diameter: the distance across a circle through its center

edge: a straight line that bounds a closed shape

exponential: a number that is a power; in other words, a number of the form a^b where (in this case) both a and b are positive whole numbers

exponential function: a relationship that changes by multiplying (rather than adding) the previous result by the same number for each interval. For example, if an amount doubles every hour, after three hours there is $2 \times 2 \times 2$ times as much. The Rice Problem in chapter 8 is an example of an increasing exponential function. It is also possible to multiply by a number smaller than 1, which will make the quantity decrease, as was shown with the water temperature (chapter 11).

fractal: a shape created by applying the same mathematical rule on a smaller and smaller scale

frame number or input number: a starting number, which a rule or pattern or relationship changes into a result, answer, or output value. In higher mathematical language, the concept of an input or starting point would be called the *independent variable*.

function: a mathematical name for a pattern rule that relates one number to a resultant number

hexagon: a polygon with six sides. Although technically a hexagon can have any length sides and differing interior angles, often regular hexagons (those with all six sides and equal interior angles) are referred to simply as hexagons.

iterative process: a mathematical process in which the result of one event becomes the starting point for the next event

kaleidocycle: a shape made from triangles formed into a tube and then joined in a ring. Also called *hexaflexigon* or *rotatable ring of tetrahedra.*

linear relationship: a relationship that changes by the same amount each time. For example, if speed is constant, the distance traveled per hour is the same each hour. The total distance traveled increases by a set (constant) amount added each hour. The graph of distance versus time will be a straight line.

measurement model for division: a model in which division is understood as measuring how many of the divisor amount fit into the dividend. So, $3 \div \frac{1}{2}$ can be thought of as measuring or counting how many $\frac{1}{2}$s can be found in 3.

pentomino: a shape made from five squares touching on at least one edge

perimeter: the distance around the outside edge of a two-dimensional shape

probability: a fraction between zero and one representing how likely an event is to occur. For example, the chances of getting a two facing up when rolling a six-sided die is $\frac{1}{6}$.

radius: the distance from the center point of a circle to anywhere on the circumference. The radius will be half the diameter.

recursive solution: the solution for finding the next term in a pattern. It is not the general solution, but might be a developmental phase for some children. The recursive solution for the stairs problem (chapter 15) might be "add n, plus the number that is one less than n, and so on down to 1. For example, for the four-step staircase, the recursive solution is $4 + 3 + 2 + 1$."

rectangle: a shape with opposite sides equal and 90-degree interior angles

row: one horizontal set of spaces or cells, or in this case, dots

scientific notation: a numerical notation in which a big number is expressed with one number before the decimal place, called the base, raised to a power of 10. The exponent on the 10 tells us how many times to multiply by 10 to get the actual value we are trying to represent.

For example, 7,654,321 is 7.654321×10^6 in scientific notation.

square: a rectangle with all four sides equal and all interior angles measuring 90 degrees

sphere: a perfectly round ball. The volume of the sphere is determined by the formula $\frac{4}{3} \times \pi \times r^3$, where r is the radius of the sphere.

symmetry: the idea of something being the same on both sides of a mirror line, that is, an image is reflected in the line

tessellation: a shape that will completely cover, without gaps or overlaps, a flat surface when used as a tiling pattern. The total-degree measure of the pieces that meet at each point adds up to 360 degrees.

tetrahedron: a three-dimensional shape made from four triangles. The plural is *tetrahedra*.

vertex: the point at which two or more edges of a shape meet

Index

About the Author

Ann Kajander received her Ph.D. in mathematics education from the University of Toronto, where her area of study was mathematical giftedness and creativity. She has published in *Teaching Children Mathematics* and has presented at the NCTM conference, the Canadian Mathematics Education Study Group meeting, and the Psychology of Mathematics (North America) conferences.

The materials in this book have been used in Ann's Kindermath Enrichment Project as well as in her regular classroom, and in courses and workshops presented to many preservice and in-service teachers. Ann has taught mathematics at the elementary, secondary, and post-secondary levels, and is currently teaching preservice teacher candidates at Lakehehad University in Thunder Bay, Canada. Her research interests include the development of deeper conceptual mathematical understanding in teachers, as well as helping them to understand what learning through problem solving and investigation really means.

As a former Canadian water-skiing champion and mother of three teenagers, Ann is living proof that mathematicians experience life to the fullest!

Big Ideas for Small Mathematicians

Big Ideas for Small Mathematicians

Kids Discovering the Beauty of Math with 22 Ready-to-Go Activities

Ann Kajander

GRADES 1–5

Share the excitement of "big" and sophisticated mathematical ideas like infinity, proof, and fractals with naturally inquisitive children in an interactive and comprehensible way—before they have a chance to be afraid of math. Kid- and teacher-friendly, *Big Ideas for Small Mathematicians* includes solid math background for the teacher, step-by-step procedures, and handouts for kids who are at the appropriate reading level.

ISBN 1569762139
144 pages, 11 × 8½
Paper, $19.95 (CAN $24.95)

Available at your local book store or by calling (800) 232-2198

Zephyr Press

www.zephyrpress.com

Distributed by
Independent Publishers Group
www.ipgbook.com

Math Games and Activities from Around the World

Math Games and Activities from Around the World
Claudia Zaslavsky
AGES 9 & UP

More Math Games and Activities from Around the World
Claudia Zaslavsky
AGES 9 & UP

"A spledidly sneaky way of countering math anxiety."
—*Hungry Mind Review*

"If I were to buy only one resource to provide myriad activities throughout the school year, I would choose this book."
—*Mathematics Teaching in the Middle School*

"This book is a treasure trove of multicultural information and fun."
—*Children's Literature Newsletter*

More than 70 math games, puzzles, and projects from all over the world encourage kids to hone their math skills as they use geometry to design game boards, probability to analyze the outcomes of games of chance, and logical thinking to devise strategies for the games.

ISBN 1556522878
160 pages, 11 × 8½
Paper, $14.95 (CAN $22.95)

"Creative teachers and parents will find ideas to stimulate inquiring young minds."
—*School Library Journal*

Math, history, art, and world cultures come together in this delightful book for kids who find traditional math lessons boring. More than 70 math games, puzzles, and projects from all over the world encourage kids to hone their math skills as they calculate, measure, and solve problems.

ISBN 155652501X
160 pages, 11 × 8½
Paper, $14.95 (CAN $22.95)

Zephyr Press

Distributed by
Independent Publishers Group
www.ipgbook.com

Available at your local book store or by calling (800) 232-2198

www.zephyrpress.com

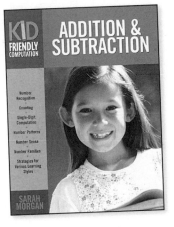
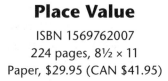
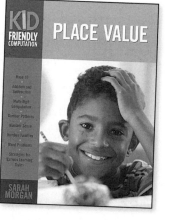
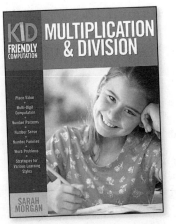